THE REMAINS OF BEING

THE REMAINS OF BEING

HERMENEUTIC ONTOLOGY AFTER METAPHYSICS

SANTIAGO ZABALA

Columbia University Press   NEW YORK

COLUMBIA UNIVERSITY PRESS

PUBLISHERS SINCE 1893

NEW YORK   CHICHESTER, WEST SUSSEX

Library of Congress Cataloging-in-Publication Data

Zabala, Santiago, 1975–

The remains of being : hermeneutic ontology after metaphysics / Santiago Zabala.

p.   cm.

Includes bibliographical references and index.

ISBN 978-0-231-14830-6 (cloth : alk. paper)—ISBN 978-0-231-52004-1 (e-book)

1889–1976.   I. Title.

BD311.Z33 2009

111—dc22   2008053629

Columbia University Press books are printed on permanent and durable acid-free paper.

This book was printed on paper with recycled content.

Printed in the United States of America

c 10 9 8 7 6 5 4 3 2 1

FOR CARMELO DOTOLO, ANA MESSUTI, AND GIANNI VATTIMO

The distinction between the Being of existing Dasein and the being of beings unlike Dasein (for example, reality) may seem to be illuminating, but it is only the point of departure for the ontological problematic; it is not something with which philosophy can rest and be satisfied.

MARTIN HEIDEGGER, *BEING AND TIME* (1927)

What now is stands in the shadow of the destiny of oblivion of Being that already preceded it. The difference between being and the Being, however, can be experienced as something forgotten only if it is unveiled along with the presencing of what is present; only if it has left a trace, which remains preserved in the language, to which Being comes. Thinking along these lines, we may surmise that the difference has shown up more in the earlier than in the later word of Being—though never having been named as such. Illumination of the difference, therefore, cannot mean that the difference appears as the difference. On the contrary, it may be that the relation to what is present announces itself in the presencing as such, in such a way, indeed, that presencing comes to speak as this relation.

MARTIN HEIDEGGER, *OFF THE BEATEN TRACK* (1950)

Our thinking, or better expressed, our reckoning and accounting according to the principle of noncontradiction, can hardly wait to offer the observation that a history which is, but in which there is nothing to Being itself, presents us with an absolute absurdity. But perhaps Being itself does not trouble itself about the contradictions of our thought. If Being itself had to be what it is by grace of a lack of contradiction in human thought, then it would be denied in its own proper essence. Absurdity is impotent against Being itself, and therefore also against what happens to it in its destiny—that within metaphysics there is nothing to Being as such.

MARTIN HEIDEGGER, *NIETZSCHE* (1961)

CONTENTS

ix

3 Generating Being Through Interpretation:
The Hermeneutic Ontology of Remnants 99

PREFACE

THE THESIS OF THIS BOOK IS THAT PHILOSOPHY SINCE Plato has not only been a "forgetfulness of Being," as Martin Heidegger explained in *Being and Time*, but an expression of Being's remnants, that is, the remains of Being. If Parmenides, Heidegger, and Lévinas suggested that "*to on*," "*es gibt Sein*," and "*il y a de l'être*," it is because Being is an event, a kind of initial generosity and gift through which philosophy began. As soon as I started my study of philosophy, reading Plato, Augustine, Nietzsche, Dewey, Pareyson, Davidson, and others, I became obsessed and astonished by metaphysics, because it investigates questions that science does not address and answers that which it presupposes. There is a universal and totally determinant attribute to things, which is existence, and to be incessantly astonished, "*philomuthos*," by this existence is what has set philosophy, "*philosophos*," on the way toward the question of what *it* is that *is*, of what it is that constitutes Beingness in opposition to beings, thinking to calculation. Calculation is the domain of ontic sciences such as nuclear physics, which concentrates on forces, reactions, and internal structures of the atomic nuclei. Thinking instead belongs to the domain of ontology, thus of philosophy, which does not concentrate on a being such as an atomic nuclei but in thinking the Being of it, in order to experience how it is that existence manifests itself in the atomic nuclei. In doing so, philosophy does not devalue the substantive world as Cartesian subjectivity, Kantian transcendence, or Nietzschean voluntarism did; on the contrary, it immerses itself in the full "thereness" of things.

There is no scientific investigation without an explicit or implicit ontology. This is the question of ontology, the "question of Being," the *Seinsfrage*, which since Anaximander, Heraclitus, and Parmenides has determined the nature of philosophy and men. This question is also the question as to the purpose, the sense, and the meaning of human life, values, and principles. It is our practical moral life that makes man ask this question. Although this problem has been forgotten for several centuries, it returned to life thanks to Heidegger's efforts at the beginning of the twentieth century. This problem was first characterized as "ontology" by Christian Wolf, after the publication of his *Ontology* in 1729, and, ever since, "ontology" has been a synonym for "metaphysics." When I was taught that this was and will always be the most genuine and central problem of philosophy, what I found most fascinating is not that most philosophers have investigated it but that all the other problems presuppose it, because it remains. That is, all those philosophers and philosophies that have not explicitly investigated this problem presuppose an understanding and remnant of Being that also determines and conditions their work. Each epoch in the history of philosophy can be alluded to in the name that a major philosopher of the period has given to the Being of entities in his research: "idea" in Plato, "*energeia*" in Aristotle, "act" in Aquinas, "representedness" in Descartes, "objectivity" in Kant, "absolute Spirit" in Hegel, "*élan vital*" in Bergson, "will to power" in Nietzsche, "conversation" in Gadamer, "trace" in Derrida, and so on. Since the question of Being implies a continuity without which there is not anything, and since as philosophers we are part of the linguistic tradition that has always investigated this question, we are obliged to pursue it.

All this induced me to take seriously Heidegger's philosophy and, most of all, the consequences of the "destruction of Being as presence" or the "overcoming of metaphysics" that he put forward both to retrieve Being from its forgetfulness and because this Being did not apply to the particular human mode of being. My teacher, either to calm or motivate my worries concerning this obsession, used to say that "to remain a philosopher means to be obsessed around the verb Being (concerning what is and what is not) because it invites you not to remain satisfied with one's own identity and to seek the entire horizon of Being—in other words, to dialogue." Although he kept assuring me I was not alone in this obsession of philosophers with the problem of Being, he showed me how few have analyzed the consequences of this deconstruction put forward for the first time by Heidegger in terms of *remnants*. I decided to investigate this problem not for sociological reasons or to put forward an effective history, a *Wirkungsgeschichte* of Being, but because the same philosophers who took seriously the consequences of this deconstruction were also observing, as Heidegger put it, that "there is nothing to Being as such" (having been deconstructed), that "Being is the most worn-out" (having been interpreted), and that Being "has left a trace" (being generational). Now, this weak or limited status of Being is not a negative aspect of it, as if its days have ended, but, on the contrary, another beginning: retrieving and destroying Being as presence has opened the way to overcome metaphysics through its remains, which are unpresentable.

Metaphysics began with Plato and ended with Nietzsche because, thanks to this destruction, we have overcome the interpretation of Being as an object that caused conceptual limitations through such polarities as presence versus absence, Being versus nothingness, truth versus error, mind versus matter, soul versus body, or man versus woman. But metaphysics cannot be abandoned, because it constitutes our understanding of Being, which we cannot escape, since it is part of what has shaped our tradition, humanity, and destiny. This is why contemporary philosophers speak of our epoch as "postmetaphysical": we are now finally aware that metaphysics is not something rigid and determining, because we have the ability to take it up consciously as our own, to shape what we see it to have been, where it will take us in the future, and even what it will become.

The ambitious "way" of this book is to outline the remains of Being after its destruction from within. This will not only indicate the remains of Being but also how to generate more Being—because the ontologies, systems, and philosophies of the past and present are only the remains of Being, which are given to us through interpretations that, at the same time, generate being. By "way" I do not only mean a path but also an attitude, a concern, and, above all, a manner of thinking. Searching for the remains of Being will build our way. Just as all ways are ways of thinking, this way is ambitious, because it springs from the primordial and principal astonishment of philosophy. These remains can be found more palpably in the work of those philosophers who have taken seriously this destruction: Reiner Schürmann, Jacques Derrida, Jean-Luc

Nancy, Hans-Georg Gadamer, Ernst Tugendhat, and Gianni Vattimo. I should immediately warn that my interpretation of these philosophers, including and most of all Heidegger, does not pretend to be a faithful interpretation of their thought—nor a substitution for reading their original texts—but rather a strict investigation of the remains of Being in their work. If the Being of being addresses itself to philosophers to the extent that they state what being is, then my interpretation cannot be a description of their opinions but must be an interpretation of Being through them.

The profound intellectual debt every disciple has toward his master is always best honored not by facile imitation or repetition but by developing one's own thought. This is only possible if the master allows such a development to take place. Distinguished intellectual educators such as George Steiner and Noam Chomsky demonstrated this. Steiner rightly explains in his *Lessons of the Masters* that the master "induces visions which are, in effect, re-visions and déjà vu," because the relation between *traditio*, "what has been handed down," and what the Greeks called *paradidomena*, "that which is being handed down now," is never transparent or accidental but instead a call that the masters, as disciples, also responded to in the past. And Noam Chomsky in *Chomsky on Democracy and Education* says that "the best teacher would be the one who allows students to find their way through complex material as you lay out the terrain." If the teacher's capacity should be *deuten*, which in German means "to point to" and which is inseparable from *bedeuten*, "to mean," then the disciple's insights must consist in responding to this call, to this indication.

My efforts in this book are a response to him whom I consider to be my teacher, Professor Gianni Vattimo, and his philosophical indications. Although I am the only author responsible for this research, it would not have been possible without his philosophy and teaching. In no way am I trying to say that I am like the dwarf in John of Salisbury's example, "sitting on the shoulders of a giant seeing more things because my sight is keener." On the contrary, what I see is not clearer or sharper; rather, as Richard Rorty genially explained, I just pursue the conversation in order to respond to an appeal. Although in this book I move beyond Vattimo's investigations, the spirit and nature of my thought is completely immersed in his "weak thought"—at least, that is my hope . . .

ACKNOWLEDGMENTS

MY MOST FOND GRATITUDE GOES TO GIANNI VATTIMO for having encouraged this research from the beginning. Without his wisdom, cordiality, and education, I would not have had the ability to find my way through this work. Teachers, colleagues, and friends such as Floriano von Arx, Pablo Cardoso, Manuel Cruz, Carmelo Dotolo, Robert Fellman, Rino Fisichella, Jean Grondin, Michael Haskell, Philip Larrey, Antonio Livi, Wendy Lochner, Ana Messuti, Richard Palmer, Mauro Piola, Jeffrey W. Robbins, Richard Rorty, Thomas Sheehan, and Ugo Ugazio provided comments and suggestions that were essential and without which this book would never have seen the light of day.

THE REMAINS OF BEING

INTRODUCTION

AS THE FUNDAMENTAL QUESTION OF METAPHYSICS, WE ASK: "WHY ARE THERE BEINGS AT ALL INSTEAD OF NOTHING?" IN THIS FUNDAMENTAL QUESTION THERE ALREADY RESONATES THE PRIOR QUESTION: "HOW IS IT GOING WITH BEING?" . . . BEING NOW JUST COUNTS AS THE SOUND OF A WORD FOR US, A USED-UP TERM. IF THIS IS ALL WE HAVE LEFT, THEN WE MUST AT LEAST ATTEMPT TO GRASP THIS LAST RESONANT OF A POSSESSION.

—MARTIN HEIDEGGER, *INTRODUCTION TO METAPHYSICS* (1935)

IF THE REAL TASK OF MODERN AS WELL AS ANCIENT philosophy has been to raise the question of the meaning of Being, since it has always been interpreted as being-present-at-hand, *Vorhandenheit*, the moment has come, after its destruction, to question the remains of Being. If Being, after the destruction of metaphysics, is no longer something present, something of which we may ask, "What is it?" then it is something that, regardless of what we do with it, remains. And it remains because ontology is nothing other than the sending of Being, *Geschick des Seins*, as presence, *Anwesenheit*. But as presence, the meaning of Being is passed along not as a property of present objects but as an essence, *Wesen*, understood as *Anwesen*, an actively being-present. The meaning of Being is no longer determined through the objective, the subjective, or the time horizon but rather through its own remnants, the remains of Being. Being, then, is that which remains, independently and separately from all predications, accidents, and qualities. But in what state is it today? Questioning Being was, is, and will always be the privileged form of philosophy. If the first question of philosophy concerned Being, could this also be the last question? In this case, would we be left only with the remains of the many answers to this question? And would this state have to be called the "ontology of remnants" and require an interpretative philosophical position, that is, hermeneutics? Let me start by outlining the meaning of metaphysics for philosophy.

Western humanity, in all its relations with beings,[1] is in every aspect sustained by metaphysics, because every age, every epoch of Western thought, however different it may be from others—Greece after Plato, Rome, the Middle Ages, postmodernity after modernity—is established in some metaphysics and thereby placed in a definite relationship to an understanding of Being. Although philosophy has been defined since the mid-seventeenth century as "ontology," the study of being as such, its nature was, is, and will always be metaphysical. The word "metaphysics" was given by an early editor of Aristotle's works who collected under that term (meaning *meta*, "after/beyond," and *physics*, "nature") all the works that came after his *Physics*. Despite the fact that metaphysics includes other branches (e.g., philosophical cosmology, theology, and psychology), for Aristotle it was meant to be the *first* philosophy, the philosophy that studied being qua being. By limiting itself only to the one-sided, objective, present Being of beings, metaphysics has used beings as the only source for truth, providing an answer to the question of the Being of beings for contemporary men and women, but it has skillfully removed from the field of investigation the problem of existence, hence, of Being. In this way, metaphysics is the history of the formations of Being; in other words, it represents the constitutive nature of philosophy, where Being has been left aside in order to concentrate on the (physical, technological, ethical, religious, cultural, etc.) manipulation of beings. Metaphysical problems are the ones that have in common this ontological dimension. This way of thinking looks beyond beings toward their grounding; in other words, each metaphysics aims at the *fundamentum absolutum*, the ground of such a metaphysics that presents itself indubitably.

What about destruction? By this term I am not alluding to the role that Jacques Derrida's concept of deconstruction played in the Anglo-American philosophical context, particularly in the areas of literary criticism and cultural studies, where distinguished theorists such as Paul de Man, Harold Bloom, Jonathan Culler, Mark C. Taylor, Drucilla Cornell, David G. Carlson, Hélène Cixous, and Annie Leclerc have developed very interesting investigations.[2] Derrida himself, in a famous interview entitled "Implications," said, "what I have attempted to do would not have been possible without the opening of Martin Heidegger's questions."[3] I am not trying to find out what happened after Heidegger's destruction of metaphysics,[4] which has conditioned our philosophical tradition, but how to respond today *from within* and, if necessary, against the grain of self-misunderstandings on his part.

It must be immediately stressed that I am not going to talk about the *remains of Being* because it has gone through a negative *destruction*, leaving nothing to Being as such. This would be a misunderstanding of the word "*Destruktion.*" Heidegger, instead of using the usual German word for destruction, "*Zerstörung,*" opted for the Latinate "*Destruktion*" and "*Abbau*" in order to avoid his term's being confused with Nietzsche's "demolition." Derrida used "*déconstruction,*" but, as we will see, he did not intend by it what Heidegger did. For Heidegger, "philosophical controversy [discussion] is interpretation as destruction,"[5] because philosophy is active philosophizing, "not a body of truths." Philosophy is not supposed to answer the question "What are beings?" but instead is meant to unfold it into the question about Being. But in order to unfold it, it is first necessary to deconstruct it. Heidegger explained in 1956 how the meaning of philosophy depends on destruction:

> We find the answer to the question "What is philosophy?" not through historical assertions about the definitions of philosophy but through conversing with that which has been handed down to us as the Being of being. This path to the answer to our question is not a break with history, no repudiation of history, but is an adoption and transformation of what has been handed down to us. Such an adoption of history is what is meant by the term "destruction." . . . Destruction does not mean destroying but dismantling, liquidating, putting to one side the merely historical assertions about the history of philosophy. Destruction means—to open our ears, to make ourselves free for what speaks to us in tradition as the Being of being.[6]

What must be destroyed for Heidegger is what covers up the sense of Being, the structures piled on top of one another that make the sense of Being unrecognizable, that is, metaphysics.[7] In other words, Heidegger, by demanding and undertaking this *Destruktion* of the metaphysical tradition, does not destroy it in the usual sense of abandoning it but instead loosens it up in order to be able to ask, in his *Introduction to Metaphysics* (1935), with a kind of complaint, "*Wie steht es mit dem Sein?*" which I think translates best as, "How is it going with Being?"[8] This new articulation of the fundamental question of philosophy is going to be at the center of my investigation, because it better suits the radical consequences of Heidegger's destruction. If philosophy cannot stop investigating Being, cannot *overcome* this problem (Heidegger used the term *"überwindung,"* overcoming, to mean a complete abandonment of the problem), but can only *get over* it (here Heidegger used the term *"verwindung,"* surpassing, alluding to the way one surpasses a major disappointment not by forgetting it but by coming to terms with it or "to what happens when, in the human realm, one works through grief or pain"),[9] then its solution will depend on a philosophy capable of recognizing the insolubility of the problem in order to come to terms with it. *When we talk about Being, we will "still" be talking about it in terms of metaphysics, because its metaphysical nature cannot be overcome, only gotten over.*

Heidegger explained that when we speak of Being, we are also speaking of the people, specifically the creative force of the people that, in its poets, thinkers, statesmen, and artists, performs the greatest assault on the whole of Being that has ever happened in Western history. Given this, philosophy will also consist in returning to the main creative force that inspired these creators.[10] But, if we assume (as we should) that the "main creative force that inspired these Men" is *questioning*, then philosophy today must clarify the remains of this questioning: hence, "How is it going with Being?" We finally have come to understand today that destroying the presence of Being was an inevitable task for philosophy. But now it is time to accept the consequences of this event, and the philosophy most suitably capable of doing this is hermeneutics, which centers its forces on recalling the remains of metaphysics through interpretation. But can a philosophy that has taken leave of the foundational illusion—in other words, a philosophy after metaphysics—really continue to call itself ontology? To continue to speak of Being and ontology is not an excessive claim, because, on the one hand, this same Being and ontology have shaped what we call philosophy, and, on the other, one cannot just abandon Being and replace it with something else, since it is the sphere through which we think. Continuing to discuss Being also keeps us committed to the metaphysical nature of the destruction that Heidegger performed, because, as I have just said, metaphysics is not something we can overcome but something we can only accept as a *remnant* we must come to terms with.

As far as the terms "remains" and "remnants" are concerned, which I will use frequently in this work, it is important to note that they will be used as variations of the same expression, that is, "the remains of Being" and "Being's remnants." While the former refers to the whole corpse of Being after Heidegger destroyed it, the latter instead indicates what is left, the traces of Being. "Remains" and "remnants" have similar origins, but there are differences in their denotations and connotations. However, I use both terms because I mean both things when I talk about Being—both Being's body, its corpse, and the traces and scraps of Being that I use to discover this ontology. The remains of Being is the condition of the ontology of remnants, and these remnants show Being's remains. I want both aspects of being—its destruction and its survival in fragments—to underpin this study.

If, since Plato, philosophers have been incapable of definitively answering the fundamental question of philosophy—"Why *is* Being, and why *is* there not rather nothing?"—hence, the "question of Being," it is because they have thought of Being as an essence, an "optical model" in accordance with an ideal, an empirical image, or a representation of objective experience. But by "becoming representation, being loses its Being."[11] Although Aristotle explained that philosophy is essentially the study of Being—the attempt to clarify its sense and the attributes that belong to it by virtue of its own nature—Greek, medieval, and modern philosophy, that is, the entire philosophical tradition, privileged only the present participle of Being, meaning a presence of Being, a modality of time that is the present. For Plato, the Being of beings resided in eternal immutable matters of perfect form, and for Aristotle, in what he called *energeia*, that is, in currents of idealization and analysis that sprang from his taking for granted of the central existential mystery. The consequence of these structures of "presentness of the present" piled on to one another are the causes, reasons, and history of how Being came to be forgotten, because it was interpreted only as presence. But philosophy, guided by the question of Being, has now deconstructed this same "presentness of the present" down to the original experiences in which the first guiding determinations of Being were acquired, in order to reveal new possibilities.

If the task of philosophy has always been to answer the question of Being, and if we fell, as Heidegger explained, into the so-called metaphysics of presence, or logocentrism, because we think of Being as an objective presence, then philosophy, after deconstructing this presentness, has finally become aware, as Heidegger once said to Joan Stambaugh, that "there is a point where one can no longer ask questions."[12] We have now reached this point. We have finished questioning, describing, and deconstructing Being, that is, asking questions about Being as presence, and the moment has arrived to interpret what remains of Being. Presentness is just one of the many forms in which Being can appear, together with its metaphysical question: "Why *is* Being, and why *is* there not rather nothing?"

The goal of this investigation is to try to find out to what extent there is nothing to Being itself after its destruction, in order to clarify what Being signifies in our present situation. This is what the ontology of remnants is all about. The ontology of remnants can only begin *after the destruction of metaphysics*. The word "after" alludes to the German term "*Nachdenken*," the "thinking that follows." And "*Nach-*" does not stand primarily for "after" but for "following upon," for the "follower of Being." Fundamentally, to engage in *Denken*, thinking, is not to analyze but to attend to or remember Being. *Bauen*, to build, which comes after the destruction of something, does not point to the notion of a novel construction but to *Hegen*, conservation, preservation, custodianship, and "looking after." Philosophy has become a response, an answer to the history of the various events of Being that have been handed down to us through a dialogue. The philosopher, after Heidegger's destruction of metaphysics, must become a listener, a respondent to the remains of Being (this is in contrast to the Cartesian and positivistic attitude, which holds the philosopher's task as grasping what is in front of her), in order to establish a relation of "audition." Philosophy, by looking after Being, which is not previously marked on a map, must think and therefore discover a path through unfamiliar terrain; science, in contrast, does not need to think, since it calculates inside already opened paradigms.

Philosophy has become a consequence *of* and *from* destruction. It is a consequence *of* destruction because we have learned that we cannot overcome the problem of Being and leave it completely aside, because it continues to appear, being the heart of philosophy. It is a consequence *from* destruction because we may only come to terms with it in order to find constructive ways to respond to it. It is important to understand from the start that metaphysics (Being as presence, objectivism) is not something we can neglect once and for all, because it is not something we can completely overcome, *überwinden*; we can only get over it from within, *verwinden*. And Heidegger's destruction of objectivistic metaphysics cannot be carried forward by replacing it with a more adequate

conception of Being (this would mean overcoming metaphysics), because one would still have to identify Being with the presence characteristic of objects. Instead, by recognizing the inevitable metaphysical
nature of Being, following Heidegger in *Nietzsche*, we can see how
"within metaphysics there is nothing to Being as such."[13] If, as I believe,
after deconstruction "there is nothing to Being as such," then philosophy ceases to be the search for Being "as an objective datum that precedes the application of conceptual schemes" and becomes the "remembering of Being that Heidegger wished to inaugurate."[14] The
philosopher, living through the history of the remains of Being, of
which he will never become the historian but only, at his rare best, a
custodian, must learn to *recollect* Being, because Heidegger's efforts in
Being and Time were not meant to arrive at a new definition of Being.
Heidegger only wanted to prepare us to "apprehend, to hear the word of
Being."

This book could have been given the title *On the Manifold Remains of
Being Since Heidegger* (similar to that of Franz Brentano's dissertation,
"On the Manifold Meaning of Being Since Aristotle" [1862]) or even
The Ontology of Remnants, but since it does not share the traditional am-
bition of ontologies, of proposing a "first philosophy," I sought to avoid
the word "ontology." Although these could have been appealing titles,
the word "ontology" could also induce readers to regard this book as
just another treatise on ontology, which is not the case because of the
"thing itself." Such a treatise would presuppose an outline of the "essence of the remains of Being" as its foundation, but this is impossible,
because of Being itself and its history. Another problem with ontological treatises is that they are never sufficiently discursive about the
world or the history, people, and politics that surround and condition it,
limiting their subject matter or, in Heideggerian terms, forgetting the

ontological difference. Although I will be using the notion of the ontology of remnants throughout my investigation, this notion has its origin and is an explicit development of the "ontology of actuality" articulated by Michel Foucault and Gianni Vattimo. These two philosophers must be credited for my use of this idea, the former for inventing it and the latter for integrating it into the history of Being.

The expression "*ontologie de l'actualité*" was first used by Foucault on January 5, 1983, in a course at the Collège de France. Although an extract of the course was published under the title "Qu'est-ce que les Lumières?"[15] the following year, Foucault published a larger version of the same text in English[16] but dropped the term "ontology of actuality" for the term "historical ontology of ourselves." In the first edition, ontology of actuality was opposed to an "analytics of truth," and in the second edition, "historical ontology of ourselves" was opposed to the "critical ontology of ourselves." Comparing both editions, we can easily observe that Foucault meant the same thing by both phrases and probably found "historical" and "critical" more appropriate, because they both could be used as opposing modifiers to the subject "ontology." Foucault never used the term "ontology of actuality" again, but he did refer to "historical ontology" a few months later in an interview with Paul Rabinow and Hubert Dreyfus in Berkeley.[17]

Foucault used this pair of terms to distinguish the possibility of choosing between "a critical philosophy which presents itself as an analytical philosophy of truth in general and a critical thought which will take the form of an ontology of ourselves, an ontology of actuality."[18] In other words, an ontology of actuality (or a historical ontology of ourselves), according to Foucault, would not turn to projects that claim to be as global as an analysis of truth (or a critical ontology of ourselves) but, on the contrary, would use only historical investigations into the "events that have led us to constitute ourselves and to recognize our-selves as subjects of what we are doing, thinking, saying. In that sense, this criticism is not transcendental, and its goal is not that of making a metaphysics possible: it is genealogical in its design and archaeological in its method."[19] This new historical ontology is archeological, because it will not seek to identify the universal structures of all knowledge but instead will only try to treat the instances of discourse that articulate what we think, say, and do as so many historical events. In other words, this ontology is not trying to "make possible a metaphysics that has fi-nally become a science; it is seeking to give new impetus, as far and wide as possible, to the undefined work of freedom."[20] Although the defini-tion of historical ontology Foucault gives here could also be used for what I mean by an ontology of remnants, it is not my aim here to inves-tigate further why he defined both ontologies the same way, preferring one term to the other. The important thing is to note that even if Fou-cault always declared that Heidegger was the author (together with Nietzsche) he studied the most but wrote the least about,[21] he did not work on the history of Being, and I doubt he was thinking about Hei-degger's destruction of ontotheology when he wrote about the ontol-ogy of actuality.

Having given Foucault the recognition and credit for first deploying the concept of the ontology of actuality, I will not be giving him any more space in this book, because he did not develop this concept in his other writings and, more importantly, because he was not referring to ontology as the history of Being.[22] This might also be why he immedi-ately dropped the word "actuality" in favor of "historical." He preferred historical ontology to the ontology of actuality because he felt closer to historicism than to ontology or, for that matter, to philosophy. Recently, the term "historical ontology" captured the interest of Ian Hacking[23] and many other pioneers of historicism, who regard history as the only truth of reality.[24] Although historicism is a significant philosophical position and tradition (which starts with Vico and develops through von Ranke, Novalis, Schlegel, Schelling, Hegel, Dilthey, Windelband, Rickert, Simmel, Weber, Spengler, Löwith, Croce, Gramsci, and Collingwood), since I am dealing with philosophy after metaphysics, this work must describe an ontology of "actuality" (I would say "remnant") and not a "historical" one. Historical ontology would imply understanding Being from a historical point of view, which would be a mistake, since Being cannot be determined by an ontic science. History has its own discourse, which depends on Being as the interpretation upon which it establishes and structures its own functions. History, by moving in a particular direction (conceived as modernization, Westernization, increasing rationality, and control through technology), thus under the shadow of metaphysics, forgets its dependence on Being. Historians have established the relation with history in a "safe" metaphysical way by positing a past radically distinguished from the present on the basis of a present object (such as the historical past or future events) that allows it to be unilinear. Thus history was determined to absorb everything in a Hegelian way, since it is ordered around a center. Instead, an ontology of remnants will regard history primarily from the point of view of the meaning of the events of Being, which are not at all linear (note that "linear" depends on a start and a finish), because, as Vattimo explains, "there is no origin located somewhere outside the actuality of the present. The event has its own thickness and certainly bears within it the traces of the past, but it is just as much composed of the voices of the present."[25]

In March 1980, Vattimo gave a conference at the Goethe Institute in Rome entitled "Toward an Ontology of Decline"[26] and, following Foucault's lead, published an essay entitled "Ontology of Actuality."[27] Since then, in many of his writings, especially *Beyond Interpretation*, he has explained the similarities between Foucault's understanding of what an ontology of actuality should be and Heidegger's new fundamental question, "How is it going with Being?" Vattimo has specified:

> I conceive it [the ontology of actuality] as the (most persuasive) answer to Heidegger's call to recollect Being. . . . For the rest, since the thrust of Heidegger's thinking leads to the recognition that Being "is" not but rather that it happens, and thus that we cannot simply return to an object, to its coming-about in presence, by dispelling the cloud of oblivion into which it has fallen, then to recollect Being will signify, for those who wish to interpret Heidegger even against the grain of certain self-misunderstandings on his part, the effort to grasp what is meant by "Being"—the word itself and virtually nothing else—in our experience now.[28]

For Vattimo, not only are all philosophies ontologies of actuality, and therefore responses to contingent questions (as Kantian transcendentalism was born as a response to the need to secure a foundation for the universal validity of knowledge, or existentialism as a response to the consequences of mass societies), but our ontological question must be formulated in such a way as to respond to the events of Being. Although my "ontology of remnants" has the same goals, ambitions, and purposes as Foucault's and Vattimo's "ontology of actuality," I prefer the terms "remains" and "remnants" to "historical" and "actuality," since the former terms clearly imply not only that "Being is" but also that we are at a point where metaphysical dichotomies are overcome because what remains, not what is, is essential to philosophy. Through Heidegger's new fundamental question, hermeneutics, and the ontology of remains,

I intend to pursue systematically what all three thinkers had in mind, not only Foucault and Vattimo but also Heidegger.

The problem for the ontology of remnants is the remains of Being. The development of this ontology will bring forward a logic of remains (a *logics of discursive continuities*) that will function through interpretation, because Being *is not* but *happens*; it remains. The logic of remains is hermeneutics. Since Being happens and occurs, the philosophical response to Heidegger's destruction of metaphysics must be hermeneutics. Not only is it the closest we can get to *An-Denken*, the only term that Heidegger used to express a postmetaphysical thought, but it is also the most persuasive way to recollect the remains of Being. In other words, an ontology of remnants needs hermeneutics, a philosophy capable of speaking of Being through its remains, which occur in events (which I will analyze in chapter 2). If philosophy is not only the expression of the age but also interpretation, a striving to be persuasive, it must acknowledge its own contingency, liberty, and perilousness. This is why hermeneutics is the right response to Heidegger's destructive demand to "loosen Being up" in order to be able to ask, "How is it going with Being?" This is from now on both the question of the ontology of remnants and the new fundamental question of philosophy.

So, since Being happens and occurs, hermeneutics is the most adaptive way to recollect the remains of Being. The term "hermeneutics" derives from a Greek word connected with the name of the god Hermes, the reputed messenger and interpreter of the gods, and hermeneutics was originally concerned more narrowly with interpreting sacred texts. Although hermeneutics had its origins in problems of biblical exegesis and in the development of a theoretical framework to govern such exegetical practice, in the eighteenth and early nineteenth centuries, theologians and philosophers such as Johann Martin Chladenius, Georg

Friedrich Meier, Friedrich Ast, Friedrich Schleiermacher, and Friedrich Nietzsche developed hermeneutics into a more encompassing theory of textual interpretation in general, rules that provided the basis for good interpretive practice regardless of the subject matter: God, nature, art, or even the social sciences. But it is first through Dilthey and then firmly with Heidegger that hermeneutics became a complete and recognized position in twentieth-century German philosophy.

It is important to remember that in his classic of 1927, Heidegger used the term "hermeneutics" not in the sense of a theory of the art of interpretation, nor interpretation itself, but rather to attempt a first definition of the nature of interpretation on hermeneutic grounds. These would be different than the grounds of epistemology or analytical philosophy, because this same concept of interpretation, after two thousand years of submission to unquestioned metaphysical paradigms, has "achieved a discourse on discourse, an interpretation of interpretation," as Julia Kristeva explains, which will finally make the "word become flesh."[29] Kristeva emphasizes this as a success, because it is a way out from what Hegel called "the desire for absolute knowledge": interpretation stood secretly side by side for all this time with this desire until Heidegger elevated it to the center of philosophy, providing a practice that finally could start loosening this entire encompassing framework. Having studied a tradition of philosophers who centered their work on the concept of interpretation, Heidegger did not regard hermeneutics as an operation of construction but as an announcement of what had already been constituted, therefore, a bringing into speech of the meaning of Being. Heidegger explained that Hermes is the divine messenger, the one who brings "the message of destiny; *hermeneuein* is that exposition which brings tidings because it can listen to a message. Such exposition becomes an interpretation of what has been said earlier."[30] In other words, hermeneutics is not a philosophical method but an attitude, the right attitude "to bring tidings, with respect to preserving a message" in order "to gather in, to bring together what is concealed within the old,"[31] thus to respond to "how is it going with Being?" Also, as interpreters rather than describers, by bringing forward an ontology of remnants we avoid the problem of finding the authentic meaning of Being or limiting it to only one terrain, because to do either would again lead to a problem of description.

If the only possible ontology after metaphysics is an *ontology of remnants*, because its question (how is it going with Being?) best suits the status of Being after the destruction of metaphysics ("within metaphysics there is nothing to Being as such"), then my duty toward Being in this work is to ask this new question through six beneficiaries of Heidegger's philosophical insights, that is, by entering into a dialogue with philosophers of the remains. But this dialogue, in order to be truly philosophical, must presuppose that if "the Being of being addresses itself to philosophers to the extent that they state what being is, in so far as it is, then our discussion with philosophers must also be addressed by the Being of being."[32] This is the only way to philosophize. It is one thing to describe the opinion of other philosophers; it is an entirely different thing to talk through them about what they are saying. Heidegger explained that we can never find the answer to the question of what philosophy is "through historical assertions about the definitions of philosophy but through conversing with that which has been handed down to us as the Being of being."[33] I do not want to suggest that philosophy has always been, without knowing it, the remains of Being, but only that some philosophers after Heidegger's destruction of ontotheology have overcome metaphysics by recognizing that Being must be worked out anew, that is, destroyed, interpreted, and generated.

In the first chapter, "Being Destroyed," I will analyze why and how Heidegger retrieved, through destruction, the question of Being and how the new fundamental question of philosophy posed by Heidegger in 1936 was also a consequence of this destruction. This will be essential to introduce the second chapter, "After the Destruction," which will expose the remains of Being within the works of Schürmann, Derrida, Nancy, Gadamer, Tugendhat, and Vattimo. Since the very nature of Being does not allow a conclusion (conclusions imply final arrangement, definitive settlement, and outcomes of an act or process), my third chapter, "Generating Being Through Interpretation," will expose the immeasurable consequences of having developed a philosophy as interpretation of the remains of Being; that is, I will show why productive interpretations generate Being. These three chapters also represent three practical examples of *destroying, interpreting, and generating philosophy*, which are philosophy's preliminary and necessary steps if it is to function after metaphysics.

Finally, let me explain that the Being I will deal with in chapter 2, as the investigation of Heidegger in chapter 1 will show, is "worn out," because it indicates Being's remnants. These remnants are all we have left after the deconstruction of our metaphysical tradition, and it is our philosophical duty "to grasp this last resonant of a possession."[34] The main characteristic of the worn-out Being is its "indeterminateness," "unpresentability," or "ungraspable-ness."[35] As remnants, it does not presence or represent anything but only answers the fundamental question of the ontology of remnants: "How is it going with Being?" It is essential to emphasize that I have chosen the six philosophers in chapter 2 because they are the first to have achieved the unpresentability of Being by following the logic of remains. Of course, it could seem too arbitrary to limit the ontology of remains to these six philosophers who, one way or another, studied with Heidegger (Gadamer and Tugendhat) or based their philosophy on his work (Derrida, Schürmann, Nancy, Vattimo), when there are so many others who are Heidegger's direct disciples (Maurice Merleau-Ponty, José Ortega y Gasset, Herbert Marcuse, Hannah Arendt, Ludwig Binswanger, Medard Boss, Bernhard Welte, Karl Rahner, Paul Tillich), colleagues (Karl Jaspers, Rudolf Bultmann, Nicolai Hartmann), contemporaries (Jean-Paul Sartre, Emmanuel Lévinas), and followers (Jean-Luc Marion, Alain Badiou). But some of these were so profoundly influenced by him that in some cases their philosophy was limited to either commentary on his works or developments in other disciplines such as theology, politics, and mathematics. At first sight, some of them could also have a place in my ontology of remnants, since a sort of similar destruction (such as Bultmann's "demythologizing") or unpresentable remains of Being (as Jaspers's "cypher") can be found in their work, but many of these philosophers were either too close to or too far from Heidegger to interpret his work beyond pure imitation, unconditional refusal, or simple development.

The ontology of remnants follows the logic of remains, that is, a logic that recognizes how, though it only counts as a used-up term, Being is all we have left and that we must try to grasp its last resonance. But this does not mean exchanging Being for something different, proposing a new predicate, or using it to explain other philosophical problems, but ultimately only asking, again, "How is it going with Being?" Because, as Heidegger said, "Being remains constantly available to us" and philosophy "must at all times work out Being for itself anew."[36] Schürmann, Derrida, Nancy, Gadamer, Tugendhat, and Vattimo are the first philosophers to explicitly work out Being anew following the logic of remains. In order to further justify and explain the logic of remains, let me explain why Lévinas, Marion, and Badiou are not analyzed in chapter 2, since initially they would seem to merit a place.

Although Lévinas, as well as Marion[37] and Badiou,[38] considered "Heidegger the greatest philosopher of the century"[39] and Being the main issue of philosophy, Lévinas did so as part of his attempt to think the other of Being, the counterpart of Being, as the title of one of his most important books indicates: *Otherwise Than Being; Or, Beyond Essence* (1974).[40] Already in *Totality and Infinity* (1961),[41] he showed how Western philosophy has "most often been an ontology: a reduction of the other to the same by interposition of a middle and neutral term that ensures the comprehension of being."[42] For the French master, ontology, through the concept of Being, gives priority to the self, neglecting and obscuring the encounter with the other. "Otherwise than Being" is not a "something," but is the relation to the other, the ethical relation that should interrupt and devalorize ontology, because the recognition of the other happens only beyond Being. Lévinas's philosophical concern is not Being but the other, the ethical responsibility of the self for the other. Although one might be tempted to consider Lévinas a philosopher of the remains of Being because he recognizes clearly that the thought of Being is the thought of that which is meaningful and that the "meaningful would be the concordant, the permanent, that which remains,"[43] he only uses ontology as a starting and contrasting point to make a place for ethics. In this way he has developed an ethics by systematically opposing ontology: while "the birthplace of ontology is in the said . . . the responsibility for another is precisely a saying prior to anything said."[44] Lévinas explained that he never wanted to renew philosophy but only to insist on the primordial intellectual role of the other, because the ethical has always been constrained, restricted, or resisted by ontology, where the meaning of the intelligible, instead, is attached to the event of being. Levinas's fear of being "attached to the event of Being, because it would be 'in itself' like *presence*, culminating in its repose and perseverance in itself,"[45] is both a confirmation that the renewal of philosophy is not possible in his opinion and, above all, an indication that he was not "working out Being for itself anew," as my ontology of remnants demands. *If Being is, and within metaphysics there is nothing to Being as such, then our duty is to find out how it is going with Being, to find its remains.*

Marion, in *God Without Being*, has gone even further than Lévinas in claiming that we must overcome the thought of Being together with its ontological difference because this is the only way to free God from all metaphysical determinations. The French phenomenologist's point of departure is a response given by Heidegger when he was asked if it would be proper to posit Being and God as identical. Heidegger's response was that "Being and God are not identical and I would never attempt to think the essence of God by means of Being."[46] Marion interpreted this answer as defining the necessity of liberating God from the question of Being, though Heidegger was only confirming his thesis of *Being and Time* and the lecture *Phenomenology and Theology*,[47] where he insisted upon the opposition between philosophy (which is ontological) and theology (which is an ontic science like chemistry or mathematics). Although reason is capable of thinking Being, Marion is certain that it cannot disclose God except within the confines of Being and therefore is limited to the ontological horizon. Recognizing this metaphysical condition, he attempted "to bring out the absolute freedom of God with regard to all determinations, including, first of all, the basic condition that renders all other conditions possible and even necessary—for us, humans—the fact of Being."[48] Although Marion could be regarded as a philosopher of the remains since he explicitly recognizes "the fact of Being," by urging us to think of God in light of St. John's pronouncement that "God is love" (since "love" has not been thought through in the metaphysical tradition), he, similar to what Lévinas has done with ethics, neglects ontology in order to theologize. But in doing so, he is inevitably conditioning theology by metaphysics—much more so than he would have had he recognized the remains of God within the metaphysical tradition. In this "theological philosophy," not only is Being not worked out anew—it is not even questioned.

Dominique Janicaud has rightly emphasized that Badiou's *Being and Event* "is the first book since *Being and Time* which again dares to ask the question of 'What about being qua being?' and brings forth an answer to it."[49] Although from Janicaud's words it seems that Badiou is also a philosopher of the remnants of Being, I cannot apply my logic of remains to him for the same reasons that disqualified Marion. He gives an answer to the ontological question by unfolding its "mathematical dimension." But mathematics, like theology, is an ontic science. Badiou's main concern in his investigations has been to escape from any historicism, and he has done so by limiting ontology to mathematics and Being to pure multiples in its proliferations. The idea that Being is like an event, a gift, a presence, and an opening from a historical trajectory of which we are only left with remnants is unacceptable for the French master, because Being does not in any manner let itself be approached but "solely allows itself to be *sutured* in its void to the brutality of a deductive consistency without aura. Being does not diffuse itself in rhythm and image, it does not reign over metaphor, it is the null sovereign of inference."[50] Although Badiou talks about "the void as proper name of Being"[51] and goes on to present it as asubstantial, equivocal to nothing, and inconsistent pure multiplicity, he believes that it must be grasped within a framework capable of containing it: mathematics. If Being is pure multiplicity, and the most formalized, most complete framework of axioms of the multiple is set theory, then philosophy should examine set theories, axiom by axiom. What these axioms say about Being qua Being will answer the ontological question, because "mathematics writes that which, of being itself, is pronounceable in the field of a pure theory of the Multiple."[52] Gilles Deleuze rightly objected that Badiou's philosophy is dominated by analogical thinking: determining its own structures in order to discover them outside itself through other discourses.[53] This objection could also function against Lévinas and Marion, because if Being is used to determine another realm of thought, then an analogy is "imposed" while at the same time "deduced" (as in *Otherwise Than Being* and *God Without Being*).

In Lévinas, Being is only a starting and contrasting point to make place for ethics; in Marion, it is the negation of the objective nature of metaphysics in order to theologize; and finally, in Badiou it is the negation of the history of Being, because ontology, as he says, cannot be "haunted by the dissipation of Presence and the loss of the origin."[54] The problem with these three prestigious philosophers is that by excluding Being or the other of Being, they are also denying Being: the exclusion of the other denies itself. But since "Being is the most worn out" and "within metaphysics there is nothing to Being as such," it can be neither contrasted nor negated, nor can its history be put aside.

My study will not produce conclusions, answers, or, in my terminology, a "remnant" of Being that would presuppose "any remnant of an in-self, which would transcend becoming, as a candidate for what endures through history,"[55] as Schürmann explained, because showing the remains of Being is a way of overcoming metaphysics from within, that is, recognizing that it cannot completely be overcome. If metaphysics could be overcome, one of the many past descriptions of Being (idea, *energeia*, act, representedness, objectivity, or absolute Spirit) or, in my case, one of the six remnants of Being (traits, traces, copresences, conversation, sentences, events) would be the correct one. But since it cannot be overcome but only surpassed through an endless continuation and revisitation, I am going to seek the remains through the new fundamental question that allows Being to appear in its different modalities.

By discussing the remains of Being, am I necessarily discussing Being? Am I taking a stand above and, therefore, outside Being? No. I am trying to enter into Being's way, path, happening, in order to conduct myself in its manner, from within its manner. The "remnants" in the "ontology of remnants" do not indicate an object but what is left or given after other parts have been taken away, used up, or destroyed. It implies continuation or being left after others have gone, and therefore it cannot be conceived as an object or even objectified. Since Heraclitus, not only has there not been any final solution to the question of Being, but it has actually been forgotten, been completely covered by metaphysics to the point that there is nothing to Being as such. However, it remains the main concern of philosophical thought. Considering that each "epoch of philosophy has its own necessity,"[56] and thus is conscious or unconscious of interpreting Being, we simply have to acknowledge that just as the interpretation of presence that was the essence of metaphysics or the oblivion of Being became the stimulus for its destruction, today it is the remains of Being that determine the interpretative nature of philosophy. If, after Heidegger's destruction of it, Being became once again the center of philosophical inquiry for some philosophers (not only the six I will study), this is not only because Heidegger found the right way to interpret it but because philosophy is only at its beginning, once again.

1. BEING DESTROYED

HEIDEGGER'S DESTRUCTION OF BEING AS PRESENCE

THE ANSWER TO THE QUESTION, "WHAT IS PHILOSOPHY?" CONSISTS IN OUR
CORRESPONDING TO [ANSWERING TO] THAT TOWARDS WHICH PHILOSOPHY IS
ON THE WAY. AND THAT IS—THE BEING OF BEING. IN SUCH A CORRESPONDENCE
WE LISTEN FROM THE VERY OUTSET TO THAT WHICH PHILOSOPHY HAS ALREADY
SAID TO US, PHILOSOPHY, THAT IS, *PHILOSOPHIA* UNDERSTOOD IN THE GREEK
SENSE. THAT IS WHY WE ATTAIN CORRESPONDENCE, THAT IS, AN ANSWER TO OUR
QUESTION, ONLY WHEN WE REMAIN IN CONVERSATION WITH THAT TO WHICH THE
TRADITION OF PHILOSOPHY DELIVERS US, THAT IS, LIBERATES US. WE FIND THE
ANSWER TO THE QUESTION, "WHAT IS PHILOSOPHY?" NOT THROUGH HISTORICAL
ASSERTIONS ABOUT THE DEFINITIONS OF PHILOSOPHY BUT THROUGH CONVERSING
WITH THAT WHICH HAS BEEN HANDED DOWN TO US AS THE BEING OF BEING.

—MARTIN HEIDEGGER, *WHAT IS PHILOSOPHY?* (1956)

TODAY, IN 2009, ONLY THIRTY-THREE YEARS AFTER HEIDEGGER'S
death, and while we are still waiting for more than twenty volumes of
his complete works (from a total of 102 volumes, not counting his correspondence)[1] to be published, there is no question that his thinking has
changed philosophy forever. This is not because there is more secondary literature on him than on any other philosopher of the twentieth
century,[2] including Ludwig Wittgenstein, nor because every philosopher after the publication of *Being and Time* had to, directly or indirectly, come to terms with his thought, including Wittgenstein himself,[3]
nor even because Heidegger invented a new philosophy, hermeneutics,[4]
able to "amend"[5] past positions. Instead, it is because he brought philosophy back to its essential realm: the difference between Being and
beings.

This first chapter is entitled "Being Destroyed" because it should raise the problem of whether the genitive of Being is objective or subjective. Is it we who are destroying Being (objective), or is Being being destroyed independently from us (subjective)? This same problem arises with the *Seinsvergessenheit*, the oblivion of Being, because the question is whether it is we who have forgotten Being (objective) or Being that has forgotten us (subjective). Who is in the driver's seat, Being or us? In order to elucidate this problem, it is necessary to put forward first the destruction of metaphysics to retrieve the "question" of Being, since "questions are paths to an answer."[6] "The question of Being attains true concreteness only when we carry out the destructuring of the ontological tradition."[7]

The term "*Destruktion*" was probably borrowed by Heidegger from Luther,[8] who used it in order to dismantle the tradition of the ecclesiastical schools that prevented original Christianity by conceptualizing it in terms of Greek philosophy (in other words, Luther used *Destruktion* to refer to a sort of critique of institutional theology in the name of the original authenticity of the evangelical message). Heidegger used it for the first time in the 1920s, in his lecture courses in Freiburg and Marburg and then in *Being and Time*.[9] My belief is that this term is at the center of Heidegger's philosophy and that all his thought should be understood as a destruction of metaphysics, because it is through this destruction that Heidegger discovered that "Being is determined as presence by time."[10] Retrieving the question of Being from the underground of metaphysics was also a sort of destruction, because it tried to polish a term and tradition in order to retrieve its ontological dimension. Although he used this concept rarely in his writings, and though it is impossible to discuss it without also analyzing the problem of "repetition," "dialogue," or "conversation," "destruction" is not an isolated word within his works; it stands for the totality of a way of accounting for a path to follow: the history of Being.

The mistake of traditional metaphysics has been to apply categories developed for the regions of objective nature to the region of Dasein. Heidegger explained that destruction in *Being and Time* did not mean "dismantling as demolishing but as purifying in the direction of freeing basic metaphysical positions."[11] But what are these "basic metaphysical positions"? What are we supposed to destroy? Philosophy must destroy all that covers up the sense of Being, the unproven concepts, the functional context, the structures piled on top of one another that make the sense of Being unrecognizable, in order to reveal hitherto unnoticed possibilities. These structures can be found in the passages in which the question of existence, of the "Being in beings," is touched on or is unconsciously implicit. Heidegger wants to deconstruct the metaphysical categories in order to recognize their negative and positive consequences, compelling them back to their forgotten source. It is from this source that we will learn how they dominate, through their grammatical third-person-singular Being, the ground configuration. Because the "the concept of Being that has been accepted up to now does not suffice to name everything that 'is,' "[12] we will have to "work out" new forms and interpretations of Being without the intention of naming everything that "is." In his course from 1927, Heidegger gave a very clear indication of the goal of destruction, showing its relation to the problem of construction in philosophy:

Construction in philosophy is necessarily destruction, that is to say, a de-constructing of traditional concepts carried out in a historical recursion to the tradition. And this is not a negation of the tradition or a condemnation of it as worthless; quite the reverse, it signifies precisely a positive appropriation of tradition. Because destruction belongs to construction, philosophical cognition is essentially at the same time, in a certain sense, historical cognition.[13]

Heidegger undertook his destruction of the history of ontology in terms of the history of Being in order to destroy the layers covering up the original nature of Being, those layers that metaphysical thinking has constructed. This destruction will bring forward a new fundamental question that will be expressed in terms of "remains" by the six philosophers I will analyze in the second chapter. But before analyzing Heidegger's destruction, it is necessary to distinguish it sharply from Derrida's idea of *déconstruction*,[14] because although the terms have much in common, the French master developed and modified Heidegger's term in a way that should be immediately elucidated so as to avoid confusion. Derrida explained that although his deconstruction "is also a thinking of Being, of metaphysics, thus a discussion that has it out, *s'explique avec*, the authority of Being,"[15] it "is not a philosophy"[16] and can be reduced "to neither a method nor an analysis."[17] When he developed it for the first time, he had the feeling that he was translating two words from Heidegger's vocabulary: "*Abbau*" and "*Destruktion*," but he still thought that deconstruction "is not demolition or destruction,"[18] because it is not reducible to the Lutheran or Heideggerian tradition, because it is political; it is an effort "not yielding to the occupying power, or to any kind of hegemony"[19] that implies the memory of the weak or the powerless—in other words, it is "a way of reminding the other and reminding me, myself, of the limits of the power, of the mastery."[20] This limit is a recognition that there will always be an unequivocal domination in our mode of thinking, communicating, and living over the mode of others, and vice versa, thus that all our thought is structured in terms of dichotomies (such as Being versus nothingness or even man versus woman) not simply opposed in their meanings but organized in such a way as to give the first term cultural, political, and institutional priority. Derrida uses deconstruction as a development of Heidegger's destruction in order to show how both the Western philosophical tradition and everyday thought, language, and culture are structured and dependent from these dichotomies. If Heidegger, as we will see, has used destruction to show that Western philosophy, in its search for the answer to the question of Being, has always determined Being as presence, Derrida went further beyond ontology to demonstrate how this same presentness also determined the referred dichotomies. Although most of Derrida's deconstructionism is intended to dig out forces of signification and undo them *within the text itself* in order to deconstruct not the meaning but the claim of unequivocal domination of the first signifier over the second, he has also developed a remains of Being that I will analyze in the second chapter.

§1. Retrieving the Meaning of Being

The "destructuring of the history of ontology," says Heidegger in *Being and Time*, "essentially belongs to the formulation of the question of Being and is possible solely within such a formulation,"[21] because the goal is not only to achieve clarity regarding the concept of Being but also regarding the question of Being, thus "to reach the point where we can come to terms with it in a controlled fashion."[22] Heidegger achieved such clarity both because he exposed the intrinsic nature of Western thought (metaphysical or representational knowledge) and reformulated the fundamental question of philosophy (why are there beings at all instead of nothing?) and because he used these two factors to bring forward a question capable of responding to the end of metaphysics. The intrinsic nature of metaphysics has been exposed through the foundation of ancient ontology in light of the problem of temporality. In one of the most important passages of *Being and Time*, he explained that the ancient interpretation of the Being of beings was oriented toward the "world" in the broadest sense and that it gained its understanding of Being from time.

> The outward evidence of this . . . is the determination of the meaning of Being as "*parousia*" or "*ousia*," which ontologically and temporally means "presence," "*Anwesenheit*." Beings are grasped in their Being as "presence"; that is to say, they are understood with regard to a definite mode of time, the *present*. . . . Dasein, that is, the Being of human being, is delineated as *zoon logon echon*, that creature whose being is essentially determined by its ability to speak. *Leigen* is the guideline for arriving at the structures of Being of the beings we encounter in speech and discussion. . . . The possibility of a more radical conception of the problem of Being grows with the continuing development of the ontological guideline itself, that is, with the "hermeneutics" of the *logos*. . . . Aristotle "no longer has any understanding" of it for *this* reason, that he places it on a more radical foundation and transcends it. *Legein* itself, or *noein*—the simple apprehension of something objectively present in its pure objective presence [*Vorhandenheit*], which Parmenides already used as a guide for interpreting Being—has the temporal structure of a pure "making present" of something. Beings, which show themselves in and for this making present and which are understood as genuine beings, are accordingly interpreted with re-

gard to the present; that is to say, they are conceived as presence (*ousia*).[23]

This passage represents the core of Heidegger's so-called revolution in philosophy, because it is from here that the "radical transformation, *Wandel*, of the human being's historical position toward Being"[24] begins, that is, the overcoming of metaphysics. Although Being is not a thing, nothing temporal, from the dawn of Western European thinking Being was determined by time as presence: it means the same as presencing, and presence speaks *of, from*, and *for* the present. It is with Plato that metaphysics begins, where the distinction of essence (whatness) and existence (thatness), the difference between Being and beings, is obscured, and Being as such is exclusively thought in terms of its relation to beings as their cause (*causa prima, causa sui*) and thus itself as the highest of those beings (*summum ens*). When the distinction of essence and existence arises, it is always the first that prevails; the priority of essence over existence leads to an emphasis on beings, on essence as what factually exists here and now. The original meaning of existence as *physis*, originating or arising, is lost, and Being is set up as the permanent nominal presence. Through this interpretation, metaphysics also becomes the history of the oblivion of Being. This oblivion had various consequences, such as translating the "substrate," what came to presence, what lies there beforehand, what lies-in-front, known by the Romans as *subjectum*. But *subjectum* has nothing to do with the subject in the sense of an "I" (*Ego*), and in the Middle Ages *subjectum* was used for everything that lies-in-front, *Vorliegende*. How did the ego ("I") get the distinction of being the only subject, the only underlying reality? Heidegger explained that this distinction of the ego appeared for the first time with Descartes, because he was searching for certitude:

Descartes was looking for a *fundamentum absolutum inconcussum*. But this can only be one's own I. For only I myself am present everywhere, whether I think, whether I doubt, whether I wish, or whether I take a position toward something. Therefore, when searching for an absolute secure foundation in thinking, the I becomes what lies-in-front [*Vorliegendes*] in an outstanding sense because it is something indubitable. From then on, "subject" progressively became the term for I. Object now became all that stands over against the I and its thinking, by being able to be determined through the principles and categories of this thinking.[25]

Destroying these layers covering up the original nature of Being, the layers that metaphysical thinking has constructed, has been undertaken in terms of the history of Being, because what is present in its presence became the completion of the extreme possibilities of the oblivion of Being. By retrieving the meaning of Being and formulating a new question capable of corresponding to its meaning, Heidegger opened the way to think Being from now in such a fashion that the oblivion essentially belongs to it instead of affecting it.

In the introduction to *Being and Time*, Heidegger immediately stated that "it is constitutive of the being of Dasein to have, in its very Being, a relation of being to this Being."[26] And in his dialogue with Professor Tezuka in 1954, he emphasized this "relation" as the "hermeneutical relation" with "respect to bringing tidings, with respect to preserving a message."[27] Although this message obviously is the Being of beings, which is what calls man to his essential Being, why did Heidegger emphasize that this relation had to be hermeneutical? This relation had to be called hermeneutical "because it brings the tidings of that message."[28] If philosophy is the way toward the tidings of the Being of beings, toward the tidings of the difference between Being and beings, and even toward the tidings of that which has been handed down to us *as* the Being of beings, then "a loosening of the sclerotic tradition and a dissolving of the concealments produced by it is necessary."[29] This is the philosophical task of destructuring metaphysics.

Metaphysics thinks Being as a whole, in the manner of representational thinking, which justifies principles such as Leibniz's principle of reason, *nihil est sine ratione*, or foundations such as Descartes' *fundamentum absolutum inconcussum*. But after Leibniz and Descartes, in all modern thinking, humans have started to experience themselves as an "I" that relates to the world in such a way "that it renders this world to itself in the form of connections correctly established between its representations—that means judgments—and thus sets itself over against this world as to an object."[30] If Being's grammatical category that dominates our understanding is the third-person singular or the present indicative "is," it must be through this same "is" that we have conceptualized for ourselves the infinitive "to be." This grammatical hierarchy, this articulated third-person-singular ontology, which we could also call "authority," has governed Western historical Being since antiquity. Determined as objectness, Being has been forgotten in favor of what is called "the condition of the possibility," hence the rational ground of beings, creating a way of looking at the world based on metaphysical-scientific authority. Philosophy must examine science not for its own sake but because it is involved in the abandonment of Being, in its conception of Being as representation where only what is made and what we can make is valued. Science and technology's objectivistic nature, which Heidegger calls *Ge-Stell* (best translated as framing, frame), the Christian dogma, "which explains all beings in their origin as *ens creatum*,"[31] and Descartes' man-centered metaphysics all have in common man's essence "framed, claimed, and challenged by a power which man himself does not control."[32] It is this rational way of looking at the world that has made unavoidable the alienated, unhoused, persistently violent state of modern technological human beings. In the globalized world, where rapid ecological and political changes have been implemented by these scientific applications, in order to increase social divisions that favored two World Wars (today we call them oil wars), the problem of Being becomes essential,[33] because it is the only way to seek the ground of these issues and because "every way of thinking *takes its way* already *within* the total relation of Being and man's nature, or else it is not thinking at all."[34]

According to Heidegger, it is essential to raise again the question of Being not only because it is a long-forgotten question and it is prior to other questions about knowledge and the sciences, but mostly because it is part of Dasein's[35] nature. But in order to raise it again, it is necessary to recognize how it must be approached by way of an analysis of Dasein, since it is Dasein that asks the question about Being. In asking this question, it finds itself "in between" the subject and the world. Dasein is not the world, the subject, nor a property of both; it is the relation, the in-between that does not arise from the subject coming together with the world but is Dasein itself. Dasein unifies the traditional tripartition of man into body, soul, and spirit in order to avoid locating its essence in a specific faculty, in particular that of Reason, of the rational animal. Dasein is not rational; its central feature (along with "thrownness" and "fallenness") is "existence," because it has to decide how to be.[36] It is this essential characteristic that makes Dasein not a rational being but, more profoundly, a relationship to Being, upon which man must decide if he wants to exist as a predator of objectivity or as a preserver of the tidings. In *Contributions to Philosophy (From Enowning)*, Heidegger also specified Dasein as "the 'between' which has the character of a mid-point that is open and thus sheltering, between the arrival and flight of gods and man, who is rooted in that 'between.'"[37] In other words, Dasein exists for the sake of Being, since it is essentially the guardianship of being. Being cannot be defined by attributing beings to it that derive from higher concepts or lower ones, because it is a self-evident concept used in all knowledge, practices, and actions. Science uses it all the time. Biology's propositions do not describe the intrinsic reality of beings, because what science in general describes is secondary to another sense of being, without which we could not even develop the most elemental natural science. Unlike the being of quantum physics, this other sense of being upon which the sciences depend is precisely the one we all understand. Who does not understand that "the paper *is* white" or that "I *am* in love"? The problem does not only lie, as Heidegger explained in *Being and Time*, in the fact that "we live already in an understanding of Being" or the fact "that the meaning of Being is at the same time shrouded in darkness," which "proves the fundamental necessity of repeating the question of the meaning of Being,"[38] but also in its contrary:

Presuming that we did not understand Being at all, presuming that the word Being did not even have that evanescent meaning, then there would not be any single word at all. We ourselves could never be those who *say*. We would never be able to be those who we are. For to be human means to be a sayer. Human beings are yes- and no-sayers only because they are, in the ground of their essence, sayers, *the* sayers. That is their distinction and also their predicament. It distinguishes them from stone, plant, and animal, but also from the gods.[39]

Instead, we do have an understanding of Being. We are those who say, and we may distinguish ourselves from stones, plants, animals, and gods on the basis of this same saying, which helps "man in his thinking to find the path of his essential Being."[40] Explicitly raising the question of the sense of Being again presupposes both a clarification of its meaning and a way to "work out adequately the formulation of the question."[41] But in order to work out this formulation, we must know what the meaning of Being is, or at least how past philosophers asked and answered this question. Heidegger, following Plato's *Sophist*, where perplexity is raised over the meaning of what we mean by Being, notices how we must start by elucidating the semantic constitution of this question: what do we mean when we use the term "being" (*seiend*), and in what sense do we speak of Being (*Sein*)? According to Heidegger, we no longer know *in* what meaning to tackle Being, because this difference between *Sein* and *Seiendes*, the so-called ontological difference,[42] has been neglected. The emphasis that metaphysical thinking has placed on Being thought exclusively as the ground of Being has made philosophy incapable of thinking this difference and therefore of thinking the relation between "identity" and "difference" in terms of what *differs* rather than how it was traditionally thought—as a static, abstract equation. The metaphysical tradition, particularly the medieval one, equated the difference; hence Being was understood as the essence of beings, of what exists (*existentia*), of the essence in the sense of the universal One that unifies everything. For Heidegger, the essence-existence distinction actually belongs to the tradition on the side of Being. Neglecting the ontological difference has increased the failure both of Western philosophy and Western civilization, because it devalued the contemplation of Being in favor of a technical use of beings. But why did science take the place of what properly should be called ontology, the study of Being?

The fundamental task of ontology is to work *from within* the ontological difference in order to remember that the Being of entities has been forgotten because, since Plato, it has failed to ask how it is that things are intelligible at all. It has failed because the tradition has understood knowledge as resulting from the effect, *Einwirkung*, of the world on a subject, even though it is actually just a mode of Dasein that is founded in being-in-the-world. The whole history of ontology has determined being in the perspective of one singular mode of time, the mode of the present; the best way to explain this is through Descartes, for whom the world consisted of objects that are already there *as such* before they are investigated. If this were the case, our thought would only have to re-present objects in search of objective accounts. But such a philosophy implies that we all have an impossible God's-eye view for which the truth of things exists in the form of a timeless presence. Descartes's conception of ontology depends upon the mathematization of the world by modern sciences, which aimed at a timeless description of the way the world really is. By being founded in being-in-the-world, Dasein, is, in contrast, essentially temporal and historical, since all our thoughts and actions take place in a temporal horizon from which we cannot step outside. Such an ontology based on the material objects of natural sciences fails to comprehend that this is just a historically specific understanding of Being as presence.

Heidegger believes every discipline—history, chemistry, or anthropology—deals with a certain area of what Being is through a certain regional ontology, thus with different sets of questions and methods. But in doing so, they are not clear about the sense in which they allow

Man to be Being. Following the interpretation of Being as presence, these disciplines function spontaneously, as if it were possible to get Man as a whole into focus as if he were like any of the other objects in the world. This is a tendency constitutive of Dasein, to "understand its own being in terms of that being to which it is essentially, continually, and most of all closely related—the 'world' . . . in terms of what is objectively present."[43] If Dasein would conceive itself on the basis of what is objectively present, then it would imply it is finished, determined, and completed, as an object might be; instead, Dasein, as long as it lives, always remains open for the future because it implies *Möglich-sein*, being possible, possibilities. In contrast to the rest of the objects of the world, Dasein has a relationship with its own Being, called "existence," because it is a self-relationship, thus a Being-relationship, as we have seen. "The ontic distinction of Dasein lies in the fact that it *is* ontological."[44]

Now that Dasein is conscious of being ontological, aware of the ontological difference, unlike other entities, it must venture into a historico-theoretical inquiry of the Being of beings. But this is only possible because of its preontological understanding of Being, which, as a philosopher, it depends upon in order to attain a conceptual understanding. Heidegger's task has been to restore man to his original relationship to Being because his conceptual understanding is not independent of what he does, says, and thinks but constitutively dependent on it; in other words, since Dasein is historical, its questioning about Being must also be historical.

The elaboration of the question of being must therefore receive its directive to inquire into its own history from the most proper ontological sense of the inquiry itself, as a historical one, that is, to become historical in a disciplined way in order to come to the positive appropriation of the past, to come into full possession of its most proper possibilities of inquiry. The question of the meaning of Being is led to understand itself as historical in accordance with its own way of proceeding, that is, as the provisional explication of Dasein in its temporality and historicity.[45]

Since the appropriate attitude toward the past is essential for retrieving the question of Being, Heidegger uses the term "*Wiederholung*," repetition or retrieval, which comes from "*wiederholen*," which can either be understood as "to repeat, reiterate, say again" or "to retrieve, to get back." In *Being and Time*, he uses the word in its first sense, but in *Kant and the Problem of Metaphysics* (1929), he explains that by the retrieval of a basic problem we must understand the "opening-up of its original, long-concealed possibilities, through the working-out of which it is transformed,"[46] because in this way it comes to be preserved in its dimension as a problem. Either way, what is essential is that we retrieve the question of Being because, since Plato and Aristotle, it has fallen into oblivion. It has fallen into this oblivion because it was taken for granted as what is objectively present, forgetting the ontological difference. "Retrieve is explicit handing down,"[47] that is, going back to the possibilities of Dasein, to ask again the question of Being, in order to overthrow the metaphysical and scientific traditions that have concealed the ontological nature of Being in favor of the ontic nature of beings. Heidegger, by retrieving the ontological question through a detailed historico-traditional analysis of the ontological difference, established that philosophy must *dialogue* with what has been handed down to us as the Being of being. Note that the term "dialogue" (originally from the Greek *dialegesthai*), which involves an *Auseinandersetzung*, discussion, if it is referred to its Latin source, *discutere*, means to "smash to pieces," and it will be used by Heidegger in order to bring back, through interpretation, what is "primary and originary, to that which, as the essential, is itself the common, and thus not needful of any subsequent alliance," because "philosophical dialogue is interpretation as destruction."[48]

Since Dasein is a "hermeneutical relation," with respect to preserving a message, Heidegger used the Latin concept of *traditio*, tradition, because its roots refer not only to "surrender" and "handing down" but also to *tradere*, to "handing over" a message. Heidegger probably chose this concept because he knew that *tradere* was originally *transdare*, to give (*dare*) over (*trans*), which would allow us to free not only tradition but also ourselves from covering the message. Being free from something "does not mean somehow pushing it aside and leaving it behind us. Rather all liberation from something is genuine only when it masters and appropriates whatever it is liberating itself from. Liberation from the tradition is an ever new appropriation of its newly recognized strengths."[49] Destructuring serves to appropriate the tradition in order to free ourselves from it. This same appropriation will liberate us from traditional concepts in which the question of the "Being of beings" is concealed; in other words, when Heidegger inquires about the question of Being, he is not waiting for a specific answer but instead pointing at a certain direction of inquiry that, although it has been forgotten—or perhaps just because it has been forgotten—is the fundamental one.

It is in section 6 of *Being and Time*, entitled "The Task of a Destructuring of the History of Ontology," that the term "destruction" acquired the status of a philosophical concept for the first time in the history of philosophy. The method of destruction Heidegger put forward is related not only against some cardinal concepts of the tradition but also against our understanding of ourselves as a reflection of what is objectively present: either in the sense of what is purely present, *Vorhanden*, or in terms derived from the world of artifacts, *Zeug, Zuhandenheit*. Although the metaphysical tradition determined human self-understanding in this secure way, Dasein cannot be adequately understood in categories derived from the world, because those categories prevent it from interpreting its innermost Being. "Ontologically," explained Heidegger, "*existentia* means *objective presence* [*Vorhandenheit*], a kind of being which is essentially inappropriate to characterize the being which has the character of Dasein."[50] Heidegger has shown that this metaphysical interpretation must be overcome, because by interpreting Dasein as a raw material of production it has reached the highest peak of objectification, because "science" was involved in the "abandonment of Being,"[51] where "everything is functioning" and where "technology tears men loose from the earth and uproots them."[52] Heidegger has gone beyond modern subjectivism through destruction in order to recover the primordial Greek experience of Being, by exposing its objectiveness.

§2. Questioning the "Worn-Out" Being

Being and Time revolutionized philosophy by explaining how beings have been grasped only in their Being as presence and by showing how every question "returns to existence."[53] Existence for Heidegger is the actuality of neither the *ego cogito* nor the subjects who act for each other in order to become who they are. Instead, in fundamental contrast to every *existentia* and *existence*, it is "ek-static dwelling in the nearness of Being. It is the guardianship, that is, the care for Being."[54] The task of destruction was primarily to try to draw the concepts of the tradition back to their original Greek language in order to find their hidden true origin, but Heidegger, by *interpreting* Western philosophy, *regressing* into the historical foundations of thought, *questioning* questions that were still unasked, and *analyzing* concepts such as Dasein, Being, and truth and authors such as Aristotle, Heraclitus, Kant, Hegel, became indirectly conditioned and determined by destruction.[55] It is this same destruction that unconcealed the actual state of Being, "a word which is of long standing, traditional, multifaceted, and worn-out."[56] The first thing he has shown us is that the fundamental question of philosophy is the question of Being; second, that man must try to answer it because he has an understanding of it; and third, that this question characterizes his essence. But, although it characterizes his essence, nevertheless it has fallen into oblivion because he has interpreted Being as presence. The problem today is that we are living in the forgetfulness of the question because we have failed to acknowledge the ontological difference. Because philosophy, until now, has endorsed the traditional ontology of presence, the new task of the philosophers after retrieving and raising again the question of Being is to destroy this same tradition, in order to turn upon an original question adapted to the state of Being today.

In a lecture course Heidegger delivered at Freiburg in the winter semester of 1941 (published for the first time in 1981), we find in section 11, entitled "Being Is the Most Worn-Out and at the Same Time the Origin," the following statements, which give us an update not only of the state of Being after destruction but also how its new state, condition, or shape (being worn out) will respond to the new fundamental question of philosophy with which we will deal now.

> For we lay claim to being everywhere, wherever and whenever we experience beings, deal with them and interrogate them, or merely leave them alone. We need being because we need it in all relations to beings. In this constant and multiple use, Being is in a certain way expended. And yet we cannot say that Being is used up in this expenditure. Being remains constantly available to us. Would we

wish to maintain, however, that this use of being, which we constantly rely upon, leaves Being so untouched? Is it not Being at least consumed in use? Does not the indifference of the "is," which occurs in all saying, attest to the wornness of what we thus name? Being is certainly not grasped, but it is nevertheless worn-out and thus also "empty" and "common." Being is the most worn-out. Being stands everywhere and at each moment in our understanding as what is most self-understood. It is thus the most worn-out coin with which we constantly pay for every relation to beings, without which payment no relation to beings as beings would be allotted us.[57]

Heidegger gave several names to Being after the destruction of metaphysics that are all determined by the way metaphysics could be overcome, by the so-called end of philosophy, by the recognition of the completion of science, and by the acceptance of the ontological difference. All these determinations of Being have the characteristic of expressing both the objective and subjective genitive of Being, because there is nothing to Being as such; Being is "worn out" and "needs man for its revelation, preservation, and formation."[58] Since "worn" is the participle of "wear," meaning affected, exhausted, or spent by long use or action, "worn out" describes something that is used until becoming threadbare, valueless, or useless. Now, is it Being that is used until exhaustiveness (subjective), or is it affected by something that has reached its threadbareness (objective)? Although we are not yet capable of answering this question, because we need first to find the question adapted to the new state of Being, from the point of view of thought, "thinking is of Being inasmuch as thinking, propriated by Being, belongs to Being."[59] In other words, the genitive says something twofold: thinking is of Being insofar as thinking listens to Being. The end of the destruction of metaphysics blends with the end of the search for Being, because philosophy, after having retrieved the question of Being through a reappropriation of its tradition, recognizes how we are only left with the many different descriptions, interpretations, and remains of Being framed within metaphysics. Recognizing being framed within metaphysics does not mean that philosophy has come to an end but rather that "the distinction, which stems from metaphysics, between theory and praxis, and the representation of some kind of transmission between the two, blocks the way," says Heidegger, "into an insight into what I understand by thinking."[60] Although it is clear that Dasein must be the "guardianship"[61] of Being at all times, Heidegger emphasizes that Being is never "used up in this expenditure," giving Being the priority over Dasein. This is also why "*précisément nous sommes sur un plan où il y a principalement l'Etre*. We are precisely in a situation where principally there is Being."[62]

Thinking has nothing to do with *reflextion*, which was a concept favored by Husserl, or with Descartes' *cogito*, which is essentially self-reflexive, "*cogito me cogitare*," "I think that I think," because thinking forms a hierarchy. This hierarchy is not based upon the authority of the scale but upon the difference of dealing with questions or problems, because "subjectivity, object, and reflection," says Heidegger, "belong together. Only when reflection as such is experienced, namely, as the supporting relation to beings, only then can Being be determined as objectivity."[63] The scientist, by thinking within a fixed horizon and boundary, which he does not see, works out solutions to problems that are objectified, timeless entities. Problems exist only on the basis of an explicit philosophical standpoint that is not a body of truths but the condition upon which problems work out their solutions; in other words, the answers to the questions science discovers are never cut-and-dried propositions as they appear at first. The questioner who thinks develops as the questioning proceeds, because it "does not have a firm line on the map. The territory first comes to be through the pathway and is unknown and unreckonable at every stage of the way";[64] in contrast, the questioner who responds to problems stands still and is satisfied. So what is called thinking? To think "requires that we settle down and live within it."[65] This call to settle down and live within the question also emphasizes that we have reached the point "where one can no longer ask questions" and must remain within the unfinished, just as *Being and Time* does.

The original plan of *Being and Time* consisted of two parts in three divisions, but although only the first two divisions of part 1 were published, Heidegger did carry out in the form of a lecture the third division, entitled as planned *Time and Being*.[66] Part 2, which was to accomplish the phenomenological destruction of the history of ontology with the problematic of temporality as a guide, likewise was not published in *Being and Time* but absorbed throughout Heidegger's later writings. Although Heidegger did develop in many other works, especially *Kant and the Problem of Metaphysics* and *Introduction to Metaphysics*, the goal he wanted to achieve in *Being and Time*, he said he was held back because thinking failed "with the help of the language of metaphysics."[67] After having destroyed metaphysics, we have to settle down within the language of metaphysics, because it is something we cannot overcome in the sense of *überwunden*, defeating and leaving it (for example, a pain) behind, but only in the sense of *verwindung*, recovering, twisting, or incorporating (learning to live with it). "Overcoming is worthy only when we think about incorporation."[68] To overcome metaphysics means to incorporate it, to appropriate it, but if metaphysics and its question become something we cannot eliminate by answering the question, then philosophy finally becomes an "appropriation," an appropriation of what remains from the destruction of the history of Being. A "regard for metaphysics still prevails even in the intention to overcome metaphysics. Therefore, our task is to cease all overcoming, and leave metaphysics to itself."[69] In this way, the ontological difference, or the distinction between theory and praxis, will finally become accessible.

In the summer of 1970, Heidegger answered in writing some questions formulated by J. Glenn Gray and Joan Stambaugh for the publication of a collection of his writings and explained what he meant by "appropriation":[70]

> Being itself means: The Appropriation can no longer be thought as beings in terms of presence. Appropriation no longer names another manner and epoch of Being. Being thought without regard to beings (i.e., always only in terms of, and with respect to, them) means at the same time: no longer thought as Being (presence). If this happens, then the thinking thus transformed thinks the following: the ontological difference disappears in the Appropriation through the step back. It loses its decisiveness for thinking and is thus given up in a certain way in thinking.[71]

After the destruction of Being understood in terms of presence, philosophy becomes the appropriation of the remains of Being, both because metaphysics cannot be overcome and because "only what has already been thought prepares what has not yet been thought."[72] But this preparation does not have, as does the earlier history of philosophy, the Hegelian character of the *Aufhebung*, elevation, but of the *step back*. While the elevation is a mediating concept, in the sense of an absolute foundation in the sphere of the whole reality, it leads to the heightening area of truth posited as absolute certainty of self-knowing knowledge. Instead, the step back indicates the realm that until now has been forgotten and from which the essence of Being becomes worthy of thought. This realm is the ontological difference. The step back goes from this unthought difference "into what gives us thought,"[73] and it does not "consist in a historical return to the earliest thinkers of Western philosophy."[74] What gives us thought, or "the matter of thinking," is always Being, the Being of beings: "Being remains constantly available to us."[75]

The innovation of having destroyed metaphysics consists in appropriating the ontological difference in order to "enter what has been. In that metaphysics perishes, it *is* past. The past does not exclude, but rather includes."[76] It is essential to understand that the matter of thinking, thus Being, remains even though its traditional metaphysical interpretation has come to an end. But this end is not null and void but rather the beginning of an accomplishment, because accomplishing means to unfold something into the "fullness of its essence, to lead it forth into this fullness—*producere*. Therefore only what already is can be accomplished. But what 'is' above all is Being."[77] Heidegger's main point is that "*Es gibt*": "there is Being—not beings—only insofar as truth is."[78] This "it" that "gives" is Being itself, because it is Being that grants its truth. Granting is donation, and "as the gift of this 'it' gives, Being belongs to giving. As a gift, Being is not expelled from giving."[79] The meaning of giving is determined by what is sent forth in destining, because when Plato, for example, represented Being as idea or Nietzsche as will to power, these were not descriptions advanced by chance but rather "words of Being as answers to a claim which speaks in the sending concealing itself, in the 'there is, It gives, Being.' "[80] But what does this "It" mean? The "It" that gives in "It gives Being" "proves to be Appropriation."[81] In other words, if the matter at stake here (Being), which we must think prohibits our speaking of it by way of descriptive objective statements, then Being can only be brought before us as the event of Appropriation. Heidegger justifies all this by explaining how "Appropriation means a transformed interpretation of Being which, if it is correct, represents a continuation of metaphysics,"[82] because, as I already explained, metaphysics cannot be abandoned like an old, worn-out garment. On the contrary, it is precisely *as* an old, exhausted, worn-out garment that Being continues to be Appropriated. It is important to take into consideration that Appropriation is not an encompassing general concept under which Being (and time) can be logically subsumed but is rather the form, without the relation of Being to beings, with which to trace Being back from its oblivion.

Heidegger is certain that the last saving grasp of philosophy will always be "aimed at the most worn-out—at Being. Therefore Being can never become worn-out to the point of complete exhaustion and disparagement,"[83] because the understanding of Being will always belong to Dasein. In this way, the twofold excluding possibility between Being and Nothingness in the fundamental question of metaphysics—why are there beings at all instead of nothing?—finishes by favoring Being, because it is Being that first "lets every Being as such originate. Being first lets every Being be, that means to spring loose and away, to be a Being, and as such to be itself."[84] Philosophy is not an issue regarding the possibility that one side might be but is rather the condition, amount, or state of Being. Having said this, in order to think Being without regard for metaphysics, thus without beings, in its actual worn-out state, it is necessary to modify the fundamental metaphysical question in such a way as to properly question Being after its destruction in terms of appropriation.

Heidegger, in the preface to the seventh German edition of *Being and Time* in 1953, after claiming that "the question of Being is to move our Dasein," specifies that for an "elucidation of that question the reader may refer my *Introduction to Metaphysics*."[85] This text represents the lecture course that he delivered at the University of Freiburg in the summer semester of 1935. It is important to remember that Heidegger, among the dozens of manuscripts of lecture courses he held over the years of his teaching career, chose in 1953 to present this one first for general publication. Contrary to many distinguished interpreters of Heidegger, I believe that this is both the most significant of Heidegger's texts after *Being and Time* and the essential text of *Being and Time*. Although in the 1927 magnum opus the central concern is the question of Being, it is in the 1936 text (as Heidegger himself indicated in the preface to the seventh edition) that this same question is finally "elucidated."

The main concern of *Introduction to Metaphysics* was to ask: how is it going with Being "at the present"[86] for us and with our understanding of Being? Although in this text he does not use the term "*abgegriffen*," "worn out," or any variant of it to characterize Being's state, Heidegger writes that Nietzsche is "entirely right when he calls the 'highest concepts' such as Being 'the final wisp of evaporating reality,' "[87] because Being is, after all, almost like nothing after metaphysics. But why does Being remain a "vaporous" word for us? Heidegger specifies that what matters is not that the meaning of Being remains worn out for us but rather that we have forgotten, fallen out of what this word was saying. But since the task of philosophy after its destruction is the appropriation, "the ameliorating continuation of what has been, by means of what has been,"[88] it is necessary to *wider-holen*, repeat and retrieve, the beginning of our historical-spiritual Dasein in order to transform it in another beginning. But in order to do this, it is necessary to recognize not only that Being "can never become worn-out to the point of complete exhaustion and disparagement" but most of all that precisely in this extremity of the desired annihilation that Being appears as something "unprecedented and untouched, from out of which stem all beings and even their possible annihilation."[89]

As the fundamental question of metaphysics, we ask: "Why are there beings at all instead of nothing?" In this fundamental question there already resonates the prior question: how is it going with Being? What do we mean by the words "to be," Being? In our attempt to answer, we run into difficulties. We grasp at the ungraspable. Yet we are increasingly engaged by beings, related to beings, and we know about ourselves "as beings." Being now just counts as the sound of a word for us, a used-up term. If this is all we have left, then we must at least attempt to grasp this last remnant of a possession. This is why we asked: how is it going with the word Being?[90]

Heidegger has raised this prior question (how is it going with Being?)[91] out from the fundamental question of metaphysics (why are there beings at all instead of nothing?), because Being and the understanding of Being are not a present-at-hand fact but "the fundamental happening, the only ground upon which historical Dasein is granted in the midst of beings that are opened up as a whole."[92] If this were not the case, then Being could be opposed to Nothing within the traditional metaphysical question, leaving aside the history of Being. But Being cannot be opposed to something: even if it appears as an empty word with an evanescent meaning, it still proves to be the most worthy of questioning in the extremity of the desired annihilation, because it "is the most worn-out and at the same time the origin."[93] By being the origin, Being is the power that still today sustains and dominates all our relations to beings as a whole, and it must be experienced anew in the full breadth of its possible essence if we want to set our historical Dasein to work as historical, since "the essence of Being is intimately linked to the question of who the human being is."[94]

One would be tempted to believe that by extracting from the fundamental question of metaphysics the prior question, *Vor-frage*, Heidegger would be settling it outside the main question as something secondary. Actually, the preliminary question does not stand outside the fundamental question at all but is "the hearth-fire that glows in the asking of the fundamental question, the hearth at the heart of all questioning." Only in this way may we restore the historical Dasein back to "the power of Being that is to be opened up originally."[95] Thus we are solving the problem as to whether the genitive of Being is objective or subjective, because putting Being in the driver's seat (in the prior question), almost as a personal agent, confirms that "we are precisely in a situation where principally there is Being." In other words, since "language is the house of Being [and in this home] human beings dwell,"[96] Being remains the fundamental concern of Dasein. What matters is to bring out the Being of beings since this is what calls "him to its essential Being."[97] This call consists in preserving the message, and the new question, by questioning the state, the ongoing state of Being, continues Dasein's call to "bring tidings." Dasein, by being the guardianship, that is, the one who cares for Being,[98] should not oppose it to Nothing but dwell in the nearness of Being, because philosophy does not have an object as sciences do. It is important to keep in mind that this destruction of metaphysics did not imply an end of the relation of thinking to Being or of subject to object but only the admission that when "we determine how Being and thinking stand opposed to each other, we are working with a well-worn schema."[99] If Heidegger's destructuring goal was to expose this "well-worn" schema (metaphysics) in order to formulate the prior question in such a way as to unfold, preserve, and maintain itself within the history of Being, then philosophy will "preserve its own historical import" and by "pursuing it, we will once again focus on the saying of Being."[100] Through this question we will continue both the most intrinsic classical problem of philosophy and Dasein's distinctive concern of guarding, preserving, and saying the message of Being, which is what it also calls its essential Being.

"Philosophy, concludes Heidegger, is a happening that must at all times work out Being for itself anew."[101] Working out Being anew is the essential obligatory task of Dasein, because if there were no indeterminate meaning of Being, or if we did not understand what this meaning signifies, there would be no language at all. Dasein is not only distinguished by the fact that in its very Being, Being is an issue for it, but mostly that through its comprehension it becomes the manifestation of Being. It is always a matter of naming Being, which is not a thing but a verb. In other words, if "our essence would not stand within the power of language, then all beings would remain closed off to us—the beings that we ourselves are, no less than the beings that we are not."[102] The fact that Being by now just counts as "a used-up," "worn-out" term for us, that "this is all we have left," and that we must at least attempt to grasp this last remnant of a possession" signifies that Being remains philosophy's main concern, especially after being destroyed, because it becomes unpresentable, indeterminable, and ungraspable. Heidegger's destruction did not destroy but instead set us free into the *Ereignis*, the happening or event of Being.

2. AFTER THE DESTRUCTION

THE REMAINS OF BEING

IT IS ONE THING TO DETERMINE AND DESCRIBE THE OPINION OF PHILOSOPHERS.
IT IS AN ENTIRELY DIFFERENT THING TO TALK THROUGH WITH THEM WHAT THEY
ARE SAYING, AND THAT MEANS, THAT OF WHICH THEY SPEAK. THUS, IF WE ASSUME
THAT THE BEING OF BEING ADDRESSES ITSELF TO PHILOSOPHERS TO THE EXTENT
THAT THEY STATE WHAT BEING IS, IN SO FAR AS IT IS, THEN OUR DISCUSSION WITH
PHILOSOPHERS MUST ALSO BE ADDRESSED BY THE BEING OF BEING.

—MARTIN HEIDEGGER, *WHAT IS PHILOSOPHY?* (1956)

FOR MANY INTERPRETERS OF HEIDEGGER, HIS GESTURE OF
raising again the fundamental problem of Being should not be understood only as the repetition of the forgotten inauguration, origin, *anfang*
of thought but also as evidence that he was searching for the original
experience of Being. This original Being would signify that behind the
Greek language there is another "unthought language" that presupposes
an archioriginary intactness that has been forgotten and that we should
appropriate. Such a Being would represent a founding and controlling
principle. If this were the case, then Heidegger was actually looking for
the one and only adequate description of the meaning of Being, because the notion of Being as presence handed down to us by metaphysics and any new understanding of it in the future would be incomplete,
partial, and somehow inadequate. Thus the prior question would be the

only right way to describe Being as it is *really* given, and all the other interpretations, including the metaphysical one, would be erroneous. But as some attentive readers of Heidegger have pointed out, namely Otto Pöggeler, Robert B. Pippin, and Gianni Vattimo,[1] this is not the case, because Heidegger also extensively criticized the conception of truth as correspondence—*veritas est adaequatio rei et intellectus*—which presupposes this same idea of Being as *Grund*, as an insuperable first principle that reduces all questioning.[2] This meditation on the insufficiency of the idea of truth as the correspondence of judgment to the thing that confirms it is not the only proof that Heidegger could not have been searching for an originary Being; there is also his constant emphasis on philosophy's need to "work out Being for itself anew"[3] because "truth happens only by establishing itself in the strife and space it itself opens up."[4] If Heidegger criticized this truth formulation that implies an originary Being, suggesting that truth is a happening and that Being must be worked out "anew," then he could not believe in an originary first Being that should be found; this would presuppose the same truth formulations he criticized. If the so-called turn after *Being and Time* is not taken literally,[5] it becomes clear that his ontology cannot in any way be taken for a kind of existentially phrased neo-Kantianism where the structure of reason falls into the thrownness and finitude of Dasein's project, becoming the correct vision of the original, first, or even natural Being. It is not the authentic, original, or true Being that is at stake here but, on the contrary, the thought of Being. It is the thought of Being that Heidegger recovered from oblivion. The essential philosophical factor here is not that the originary Being has occurred, not even in the earliest moments of Greece, but that it continues to happen.

What has induced many interpreters to imagine Heidegger's search for the originary Being is the oblivion of the ontological difference. But if we read carefully, this oblivion only refers to the difference between Being and beings, not to a forgetfulness of an origin that must be re-appropriated, because the "oblivion of Being is oblivion to the difference between being and the Being."[6] Being's destiny begins with the oblivion because it is the thought of Being that has been forgotten, not a particular Being, and this thought consisted in forgetting the difference. The "destiny of Being begins with the oblivion of being so that Being, together with its essence, its difference from the Being, keeps to itself. The difference collapses. It remains forgotten."[7]

"To remain, says Heidegger, means: not to disappear, thus, to presence";[8] in other words, remains are those pieces, scraps, and fragments that are not only left after use but also survive. The enduring, surviving Being for Heidegger is not the strongest but, on the contrary, as we have seen, is the *worn out*, the used-up term, a vaporous word of which there is nothing as such and that is never exhausted in the present of its inscription. We may now overcome metaphysics, because Being can be experienced as "something forgotten only if it is unveiled along with the presencing of what is present; only if it has left a trace, which remains preserved in the language, to which Being comes."[9] Derrida has rightly explained that:

The remainder *is* not, it is not a Being, not a modification of that which is. Like the trace, the remaining offers itself for thought before or beyond Being. It is inaccessible to a straightforward intuitive perception (since it refers to something wholly other, it inscribes in itself something of the infinitely other), and it escapes all forms of prehension, all forms of monumentalization, and all forms of archivation. Often, like the trace, I associate it with ashes: remains without a substantial remainder, essentially, but which have to be taken account of and without which there would be neither accounting nor calculation, nor a principle of reason able to give an account or a rationale (*reddere rationem*), nor a Being as such. That is why there are *remainder effects*, in the sense of a result or a present, idealizable, ideally iterable residue.[10]

As we can see from this passage, the remains of Being we will encounter in Derrida will be the "trace," which not accidentally has much in common with Heidegger's concept of the worn out: both refer to something else; both have been used and are remainders. All six varieties of the remains of Being that I will bring forward will resemble Heidegger's worn-out Being, because they are all an understanding of Being after the destruction of metaphysics. Also, note from the last line of Derrida's passage the reference to the "result" or the "present residue," because this anticipates the theme of my third chapter, where not only do interpretations generate new Being, as I have said, but these same remains of Being also generate new interpretations, just as Heidegger's worn-out Being generated, indirectly, the Being recognizable in the following six authors. Although the remains of Being have the duty to recall Being, the origin, they will also "effect" more potential interpretations. This is why Derrida believes that the "dispersion of the remainder effects . . . different interpretations."[11] But in order to pursue this theory of interpretation further, philosophy must first recall the remains of its origin, hence Being.

In this second chapter, I will seek the remains of Being, the state in which Being addresses itself, through six philosophers who worked after Heidegger's destruction of metaphysics, under the admonition that philosophy must work out Being for itself anew. In other words, philosophy must apply the fundamental question I mentioned earlier—

how is it going with Being?—in order to understand the way Being happens. Because, as Heidegger said, Being addresses itself to philosophers to the extent that they express what Being is, my discussion with these philosophers must follow the question of how it is going with Being within their works. In this way, we will both know the remains of Being and how "Dasein says Being."

The following six worn-out conceptions of Being are consequences of Heidegger's destruction and, most of all, of newly worked out Being, since productive interpretations generate Being (as I will analyze and develop in the third chapter). It is important to emphasize the ontological meaning of the term "generation," because the remains of Being will actually be "generational," that is, offspring at the same stage of descent from a common ancestor. A generation is not something concluded but rather the process of bringing into Being, reproducing progenies indeterminately. Although it is only through interpreting the end of metaphysics that Being is newly generated, this same new generation of Being only occurs within metaphysics, thus as the remains of Being, because, as we have seen, metaphysics can only be overcome through "incorporation."[12] From Schürmann, Derrida, Nancy, Gadamer, Tugendhat, and Vattimo I will render this incorporation, that is, the remains of Being, in such a way that each Being will be worked out for itself anew. As I explain in the introduction, most of these authors both have taken very seriously Heidegger's destruction of metaphysics and have gone beyond imitation or repetition, generating new Being, new ways to put forward the remains of Being.[13] Although all of these authors (except Nancy) have devoted entire books to Heidegger, I will not pay particular attention to their specific interpretations of Heidegger (such as Derrida's *Of Spirit: Heidegger and the Question* or Gadamer's *Heidegger's Ways*), instead focusing on their philosophy of the remains of Being, which is, nevertheless, dependent on Heidegger's notion of destruction. Also, note that the remains of Being do not follow any sequential order, hierarchy, or chain in order to produce a scale, as with the Aristotelian categories; neither can they be catalogued within a system or an effective history, because, although the remainders refer to Being, this reference is dependent on generational interpretations. These six remains do not follow a logic (or scale) of quantity, quality, or any other determination of Being but only the *ontology of remnants*. This ontology, as I have said, depends only on the remnants "from" and "of" Being, that is, "from" the generations that have produced it and "of" the generations it will produce. Although this difference will become clearer by way of the following sections, it is the only justification that can be given to the "order" in which I situated each philosopher's remnant. As we can see, this logic does not depend on a scale or structure but only on its own happening of and from its own self-determination, constituted by Heidegger's destruction.

§3. Schürmann's Traits of Economical Anarchies

Our question—how is it going with Being?—receives an articulated response in Reiner Schürmann's work, because he centered his philosophy mainly on the consequences of Heidegger's destruction of metaphysics, where "measures remain, although radically temporalized, but the standards perish."[14] The remains of Being in Schürmann can be found in the differences between metaphysical and postmetaphysical thinking. Unlike Derrida, Schürmann sharply distinguishes between "destruction" and "deconstruction." While the subject matter of the first was philosophical systems and its goal was to retrieve the thought from which each of the inherited ontologies was born, the subject matter of the second "is provided by the constellations of presencing that have succeeded one another throughout the ages," and its goal is to uproot Being "from domination by the idea of finality, the teleocracy where it has been held since Aristotle."[15] As we will see, deconstruction is more than just the method for stepping back from the historical modalities of presence (*Anwesenheit*) to presencing itself as the "event" (in order to assign metaphysical grounding a site of competence within contingent fields and epochs). It also recalls that its own legitimation is always referring to something else, making the ontological difference the central issue.

The ontological difference of metaphysical thought is such that it allowed "the securing of foundations for beings, reasons for propositions, [and] a 'why' for action."[16] These securing foundations are nothing but a posteriori objectifications applied through metaphysical standards of Being such as "man," "God," or the "principle of ideality." After deconstructing metaphysics, the ontological difference becomes a distinction between "presence" and "letting presence"; in other words, it is a difference that does not ground anything. Instead "of a ground," says Schürmann, "it leads to an abyss, instead of pointing to the 'why' (*warum*) of phenomena, it points to their 'since' (*weil*)."[17] This abyss will overcome the traditional teleological measures that have assigned ends to whatever is to be known or done, and it also constitutes the very strength and essence of Western civilization, because it is placed under the control of metaphysical "stamps" (*Prägungen*) that Schürmann specifically called "epochal principles." Although in this culture philosophers have been called upon to secure end-setting and tele-thetic measures, the deconstruction of metaphysics (through the temporalization of Being) has discovered and delegitimized all the representations of measures as they undergo a displacement through their own constellation of events. Each epoch is dominated by what is "first caught" in it, by its *primum captum*, and "in each historical-cultural epoch." Schürmann explains:

> The network of phenomenal interconnectedness that always situates us anew diachronically, is a measure for acting and thinking, but it is not a standard. Although it determines every possible occurrence, it does not set any ideal to which whatever occurs is to be referred. It is not man's other. It transcends him, but more like a system of transcendental conditions than like a transcendent model. That transcendentality likens the measure to a structural *a priori*, but one that allows for *a posteriori* objectification.[18]

In this way, we objectify past epochal measures when we speak of Greece, the Middle Ages, modernity, or postmodernity, especially if they seem to yield any sort of order or canon. These canons would be in constant transition through breaks, ruptures, and divisions, because the *epoché* cannot be a measure rational to the communities it posits. Once we recognize that these epochal canons, measures, or principles draw to a close, another shape of presencing must take over from within each epochal unconcealment. Schürmann, in order to explain this change of epochal presencing and to interpret Being as the mere epochal sequence of representations, recovers, following Heidegger's *Contributions to Philosophy (From Enowning)*, the concept of "event," which also "designates the originary time phenomenon, which is the condition for historical as well as ecstatic time."[19] Since the previous quest for principles was nothing more than a quest for ultimate ontic referents, once these ultimate referents lose their credibility and philosophy has nothing else to conform itself to but the event of presencing, the remains of

Being do not designate either some noumenal in-itself or a mass of raw sense data but instead the event of presencing that implies the "end of indubitably first referents."[20]

Schürmann's originality consists in his combining the terms "economy" and "presence" into *"Anwesenheit,"* the first word to refer to the constellations of concealing-unconcealing, that is, to aletheiological constellations and later to being as it appears in a given context, that is, to beingness. But if presence is a historical mode of presencing, *Anwesen*, there must be many "economies of presence" that may be either metaphysical, ruled by an epochal principle, or postmetaphysical, thus "an-archic." Although an economy is only the fabric of relations according to which the ingredients, principles, or entities of an epoch unite, this unity does not occur as a given for consciousness but by "acting systemically on one another."[21]

The step from metaphysics (explaining beings) to postmetaphysics (thinking beings) is actually the step into the "other" thinking, the one that shows both how metaphysical grounding is always located epoch-ally and that ultimate foundations have a determinate age and where "much remains for us to think but little for us to know."[22] It is here that Being becomes the epochal unconcealedness as it arises, ever new, out of concealment. "What is permanent, what belongs to all epochs, is this interplay of *phuein*, showing forth, and *kryptein*, hiding—hardly a ground to legitimize action from."[23] It is this interplay of differences that gives and sends the various figures of epochal economies, because "difference destines, sends, time and Being. That is, the difference plays itself out in irreducibly manifold, finite, arrangements of phenomena."[24] To understand being through its economic traits is not to understand it in terms of any groundedness in entities but in terms of beingness, which, as a set of conditioning historical loci, "grounds nothing." In other words, when a historical world falls into place, its beginning automatically assigns a new economy that becomes the birth of an epoch that is not history founding but the presencing by which phenomena appear within a given order. This Being, or presencing, is actually the "synchronic emergence" within the order. As an emergence, it determines not only presence but also absence, out of which emergence takes place, because "presencing-absencing is the a priori event that makes it possible for any such order to spell itself out of history."[25]

Schürmann uses the destruction of metaphysics, the transition from a "principal economy" to an "anarchic economy" of presence, to prepare "an anarchic economy of being" that will give thinking over to its sole and unique task: "gathering up the economic traits of presence so as to retrieve presencing as such."[26] While ontic sciences study the modes in which a given era corresponds to its epochal principles, philosophy will think by complying with the economic mutations of presencing. But what does this anarchic economy look like? First of all, it is essential to understand that by "anarchy" he means "absence of rule, but not absence of rules,"[27] because in our anarchic economy thinking and acting espouse fluctuations in the modalities of presencing; that is, the only standards for feasible things is the event of mutual appropriation among entities. In this condition, temporality of the event can neither be reducible to epochal stamps nor be understood from man's projected world but only to "the coming about of any constellation of thing and world."[28]

Although the subjective command over objects has been the predominant form in the West, by responding to the principial command over the economies, Schürmann's analysis suggests that man can no longer appear in the posture of a legislator over entities but, on the contrary, must be the guard who thinks. If principial or archic economies enjoined man to master all that there is, an-archic economies enjoin us to think in the sense of thanking, of submitting to economic mutations. Man is epochally summoned to summon entities that conform to his reason in order to guard aletheiological constellations. The issue for thinking is an investigation into the history of reversals "so as to discover the traits of Being."[29]

If Being, after destruction, occurs in a groundless ground, that is, in epochal constellations of absence and presence that call upon man to exist in a certain way, then philosophy will become a "response to historical constellations of truth as 'aletheia.'"[30] According to Schürmann, the meaning of Being can be found in the "interplay of differences," thus in Heidegger's "aletheiological theory": *the theory of historical-cultural disclosures as successive epochs and modes of truth.* In this way, if deconstruction depends upon the constellations of presencing that have succeeded one another throughout the ages, philosophy must become a response to the mode in which things present are present, thus a response to the epochal order of things in which we live, which is nothing more than the epochal constellation of unconcealedness and concealment. If an entity is true as it enters into presence, then its manifestation must be its only truth, because the field in which there is truth is the difference between "a modality of presence and presencing, or between the given and the giving."[31] This aletheiological theory allows us to see how the ontic beings that imposed their economy on finite orders of presencing irrevocably vanish from preceding epochs with the rise of new constellations of truth, because "as an epoch comes to an end, its principle withers away."[32] In this constellation of events, postmetaphysical philosophy must have an attitude of readiness for new possible folds in the history of epochs, because epochal truths set themselves into work "with a leap, that is to say, in a sudden flip of historic fields."[33]

Within these new folds of constellations of truths, it is impossible to understand the origin either as the Aristotelian *arché* (the beginning that starts and dominates a movement) or as the *principium* (as that which is gotten hold of first) but instead only as a "multifarious emergence of the phenomena in a field provisionally opened by the difference."[34] If the origin of Being is a mere showing, a mere contingent coming forth, which cannot be drawn to an *arché*, then the deconstruction of metaphysics has individuated the origin as an-archic, because until now things have been frozen around a first rational *principium*. Schürmann understands Being as the epochal order of presencing that, because of its essential contingency, would simply be another way of expressing the groundless ground, the appropriating event in which finite constellations of truth assemble and disassemble themselves. This discovery of the origin as essentially an-archic depends on Heidegger's usage of the phrase "It gives" (*"Es gibt"*), which shows how Being is given differently at each epochal reversal, because the sudden advent of an new order "gives also a new modality of presence."[35]

Although a thought for Schürmann is nothing other than the dawn of an economy, once epochs introduce fluidity into a given economy, the "constellations of truth" break principles, producing broken hegemonies.[36] But how is this fluidity individuated? It is individuated, as I have said, through deconstruction, which is the method for stepping back from the historical modalities of presence to presencing itself as event. This step, however, does not come out of the blue, because it is bound by rules within history that can be indicated as the "traits of Being." For Schürmann, these "traits" are those economic mutations that, by giving shape to the event, must be "retained as the only measure for thought"[37] and, for us, as the only remains of Being. Traits, just like Derrida's "traces," are distinguishing features, as of a person's character or a genetically determined characteristic, which are discovered after a long period of time. But traits can also be those systemic features that connect epochs by indicating rules, self-regulations, and ruptures within history that traverse history:

> The originary traits of being appear in the effort of disengaging thinking from metaphysics. Hence the importance of a historical deduction of the categories of presence. It shows what happens in epochal breaks such as the arrival of modernity: a play of differences determines anew something that remains the same across the ages. But what remains the same is only a fabric of categories. This excludes any remnant of an in-itself, which would transcend becoming, as a candidate for what endures through history. The historical deduction of the categories of presence is essential not only for establishing that "thinking of being" cannot outgrow the deconstruction of history, but also for insuring that Being is not conceived as something noumenal, as quasi-divine; that it is "one" only formally, as a law of economic functioning. The first rule for understanding Being is to wrest from history the traits of *epochal self-regulation.*[38]

If, as this significant passage indicates, in order to understand Being we must "wrest" from history the traits of epochal self-regulations ("wresting" signifies obtaining something not only by forceful pulling, twisting, and extracting movements but also from within and through it), then Being once again becomes the forgotten source, the lost treasury, or even the remnant of a possession we must appropriate, as I explained in the introduction. Although Heidegger did bring back the question of Being, Being itself resists categorization and full grasp because the event of Being, specifies Schürmann, "joins presencing with absencing"; in other words, it is "Being, which is a verb . . . [that] designates the self-manifestation of an entity out of and against absence."[39] This is an indication of philosophy's obligatory task once the principal constellations of presence lose their credibility, hence after metaphysics, because it must unlearn its age-old reflex of searching for invariable principles and standards. These have always been the reference points of legitimation for praxis that philosophers used to imprint, impose, and inform; now philosophers are the ones who have only to respond thoroughly to the phenomenal disposition enclosing and situating them. Thinking becomes essentially compliant with the flux of coming-to-presence, with constellations that form and undo themselves following the event of appropriation.

§4. Derrida's Treasures of Traces

At the beginning of *Of Grammatology*, one of his most significant books, Jacques Derrida explicitly points out, referring to Heidegger, that "one does not leave the epoch whose closure one can outline," because "the movements of belonging or not belonging . . . are too subtle, the illusion in that regard are too easy, for us to make a definite judgement."[40] If philosophy is inherited by a language and, at the same time, inhabited by this same language, the philosopher must not avoid this problem but, on the contrary, work within it. Philosophy "always reappropriates for itself the discourse that de-limits it"[41] because, as Heidegger explained, we always conduct our activities in an understanding of Being that we do not comprehend; in other words, philosophy is de-limited by its own question, which comprehends (since we always have a vague, average understanding of Being) but cannot fix conceptually through communicative meaning. "It remains," says Derrida, "that the meaning of these 'limits' is given to us only on the basis of the question of the meaning of Being."[42]

Derrida is a philosopher who has been better able to overcome metaphysics through "incorporation" since he began to emphasize how the fundamental concepts of philosophy are all tied to the history of certain languages and how there comes "a moment in which one can no longer dissociate the concept from the word in some way."[43] This is why, for Derrida, the philosopher is above all the "guardian of memory": someone who asks himself questions about truth, Being, and language in order *to keep*. But what does the philosopher keep? The philosopher, says Derrida, "keeps keeping, '*garde*,'"[44] because one cannot keep oneself. Keeping is always confided to the other, just as Hermes was the divine messenger, the one who brought the message of destiny, with respect to preserving a message in order to gather in, to bring to others what is concealed within the old.

> When one writes, one accumulates as much as possible a certain reserve, a treasury of traces, whatever they may be, whatever they're worth; but for them to be more safely protected or guarded, one confides them to the other. If one writes them, if one puts them on tape or on paper, or simply in the memory of others, it's because one cannot keep oneself. The keeping can only be confined to the other. And if one wants to keep everything in oneself, at that moment it is death, poisoning, intoxication, turgidity. To keep means to give, to confide: to the other.[45]

This treasury of traces is Derrida's idea of philosophy that can be achieved through deconstruction, which is a "thinking of Being, of metaphysics, thus a discussion that battles with, 's'explique avec,' the authority of Being."[46] Being seems to be what we "keep keeping," or even a "treasure as a treasury of traces," since metaphysics can only be overcome through incorporation. But more than using deconstruction in order to analyze the system, foundation, or architectural structure of traditional ontology, Derrida's philosophical goal was also, among other things, to individuate another writing of the question of Being, which for us means more "remains of Being."

As I pointed out in the first chapter, although Derrida's notion of deconstruction is quite different from Heidegger's destruction, he explained several times how all his work would not have been possible without the German master's questions and, most of all, without "the difference between Being and beings, the ontico-ontological difference such as, in a way, it remains unthought by philosophy."[47] The fundamental problem for the French philosopher is to find a way to explicate what has remained unthought in philosophy, hence what is unveiled along with the presencing of what is present. But this is only possible, as Heidegger indicated, if this unthought thought "has left a trace to which Being comes"; therefore, all the determinations, names, or interpretations of this trace belong to the Being that shelters the trace but not to the trace itself. "There is no trace *itself*, no *proper* trace" says Derrida, since the ontological difference cannot appear as such.

The trace of the trace which (is) difference above all could not appear or be named *as such*, that is, in its presence. It is the *as such* which precisely, and as such, evades us forever. Thereby the determinations which name the difference always come from the metaphysical order. This holds not only for the determination of difference as the difference between presence and the present (*Anwesen/*

Anwesend), but also for the determination of difference as the difference between Being and beings. If Being according to the Greek forgetting which would have been the very form of its advent, has never meant anything except beings, then perhaps difference is older than Being itself.[48]

Derrida, through an original and detailed analysis of Heidegger's 1946 essay "Anaximander's Saying," reached the conclusion (which is actually the start of his philosophical investigation) that difference must be older than Being because Being has never meant anything other than beings. Not only does the oblivion of Being belong to the essence of Being, but the dawn of the destiny of Being is nothing other than this same oblivion. Being keeps to itself its own oblivion together with its distinction from beings.

Thus the distinction collapses, and the two differences, what is present and presencing, *das Anwesende und das Anwesen*, reveal themselves without distinction, as simple presence. This presence, explains Derrida, "far from being, as is commonly thought, *what* the sign signifies, what a trace refers to, presence, then, is the trace of the trace, the trace of the erasure of the trace."[49] The *erased* distinction and the *traced* trace, or better, the early trace of difference and that which maintains it as a trace, belong to the tradition of metaphysics but not to the trace itself. This is why Derrida, in the passage quoted above, insists upon the idea that this trace cannot be named because the "trace is not a presence but the simulacrum of a presence that dislocates itself, displaces itself, refers itself, it properly has no site—erasure belongs to its structure."[50]

Metaphysics maintains the mark of what it has lost through the erasure of the early trace of difference, but this early trace has become by now the same tracing through metaphysics, because "the present becomes the sign of the sign, the trace of the trace."[51] If the presence (or metaphysics) has become the function of generalized reference in which the early trace of difference is sheltered and retained, the fundamental problem for Derrida is to find a way to name the trace that has vanished in the destiny of Being or that "unfolds," as Heidegger said, "in world-history as Western metaphysics."[52] To name the difference of the essence of Being (in the beginning of Being's oblivion) signifies reference to something beyond the history of Being, which, by being beyond language, becomes also outside texts. How can we name what is other than the texts of Western metaphysics? If the trace quickly vanishes through the metaphysical destiny of Being, escapes every determination and every name it could receive, and ends by being sheltered, dissimulated in these same names without appearing in them as the trace itself, then the trace will become that which "threatens the authority of the *as such* in general, of the presence of the things itself in its essence."[53] Although the trace is not a substance, a present existing thing, but is instead a process that is changing all the time, there "is no presence without trace and no trace without a possible disappearance of the origin of the said trace."[54]

Derrida's philosophical operation here was both to explain that the limitation of the sense of Being within the field of presence (that is, Western metaphysics) was produced through the domination of a linguistic form "*derivative* with regard to difference" and to question "what constitutes our history and what produced transcendentality itself."[55] For Derrida, the sense of Being is not transcendental or transepochal but "a determined signifying trace," because the ontological difference and its grounds are not only not originary but actually derivative with regard to what he calls "*différance*," "differance." Derrida has altered the French word *différence* (difference) by substituting an *a* for the *e*, producing a modification that remains purely graphic: "it is read, or it is written, but it cannot be heard."[56] But why is this useful for Derrida's deconstruction? It "marks the *movement* of this unfolding"[57] of the ontological difference and allows him to refer to an order (of the trace) that no longer belongs to sensibility nor intelligibility, to the ideality that is not fortuitously affiliated with the objectivity of metaphysical understanding. In other words, this is an order that resists the founding "opposition of philosophy between sensible and intelligible."[58] *Différance* is not only what in the presence of the present does not present itself, hence, a way to name the trace that does not present itself, but is also the same condition that exposes what is present, because

> the (pure) trace is differance. It does not depend on any sensible plentitude, audible or visible, phonic or graphic. It is, on the contrary, the condition of such a plenitude. Although it *does not exist*, although it is never a *being-present* outside of all plenitude, its possibility is by rights anterior to all that one calls sign (signified/signifier, content/expression, etc.), concept or operation, motor or sensory. This differance is therefore not more sensible than intelligible and it permits the articulation of signs among themselves within the same abstract order—a phonic or graphic text for example—or between two orders of expression.[59]

The trace serves Derrida as a way to overcome the very condition of the illusion of the presence of Being, which presupposes that any being, element, or concept can be present in and of itself, that is, referring only to itself because "no element can function as a sign without referring to another element which itself is not simply present. . . . There are only, everywhere, differences and traces of traces,"[60] because each being appearing on the scene of presence, just like the signified concept, is always related to something other than itself or inscribed in a "system within which it refers to the other, to other concepts, by means of the systematic play of differences. Such a play, *différance*, is thus no longer simply a concept, but rather the possibility of conceptuality."[61] Experience, for Derrida, is always an experience of trace.

By deconstructing the originary presence of Being, naming, and individuating the nonpresent (*différance*) difference from the ontological difference as "something that remains without remaining, which is neither present nor absent, which destroys itself, which is totally consumed, which is a remainder without remainder,"[62] Derrida has responded to our question, "How is it going with Being?" He has named the remains of Being "traces," "cinders," and "ashes,"[63] creating a new "order" that no longer belongs to Being as presence, although "it transports it" and "includes ontotheology."[64]

§5. Nancy's Copresences of Singular Plurals

Before showing the remains of Being in the thought of Jean-Luc Nancy, and therefore how he responds to our question, I must outline how philosophy for the French master is not authentic "philosophizing" when it limits itself to undertaking a classical problem from its tradition but only when "it grasps the fact that existence unfolds in the midst of an understanding of Being."[65] In other words, the gesture of thinking after metaphysics does not consist in a theoretical investigation where philosophy would be decisive for the understanding of Being. On the contrary, it is itself a gesture of the existent as such. The ontological difference for Nancy lies neither in its being this difference, nor in its being in a specific way, but only in that it is to come, to arrive, to emerge in the properness of its own event. "Being is *nothing* outside of or before its 'own' *folding* of existence."[66] Nancy, by operating a fusion between the "event" of aletheiological constellations and the "writing" of the ontological difference, has brought forward a "finite thinking of the finitude." This thinking depends upon our finite existence, because from the moment that we exist we already have not only an understanding of Being, as Heidegger explained in *Being and Time*, but, even more so, an understanding of the finitude of Being. Understanding does not mean grasping a determinate concept; it means entering from within the very ontological dimension of understanding, that is, "relating to some particular sense."[67] Philosophy is not a matter of building or constructing but of contemplating "the world, the spacing of its *there is.*"[68]

According to Nancy, metaphysics may only be overcome from the inside, because its deconstruction is a possibility that belongs to its own traditional constitution. In other words, if metaphysics is of a *deconstructive nature*, it is because it is constantly relating to its own origins. "To deconstruct," explains Nancy, "means to dismantle, to loosen up the assembled structure in order to bring into the play of its pieces the various possibilities from which it stems but which, as a structure, it covers over."[69] Although Nancy follows Schürmann and Derrida in using deconstruction to loosen the assembled metaphysical structures, his originality consists in emphasizing how it is no longer a question of destroying something in order to make room for something else, as many believe, but of "bringing the *templum* to the *spacing* of being."[70] In other words, he insists on explaining how deconstruction does not indirectly build another world, because one *always already* dwells and departs from the world: "only from within what is constituted by and on the basis of the distension of an opening can there be anything like a sense to be sought and dismantled."[71]

Nancy also calls this "distention of an opening" "existence," because before all scientific representations, religious beliefs, and even philosophical reflections there is *that*: the *that* of, precisely, *there is*. But "there is" is not itself a presence to which our demonstrations might refer, since it is always, already there, though not in the mode of "being" as a substance nor in that of "there" as presence. It "is in the mode of being born: to the degree that it occurs, birth effaces itself, and brings itself indefinitely back. . . . To be born is the name of being."[72] The essence of "birth" is that *coming* that effaces and brings itself back just like the constitution of Derrida's *différance*. The remains of the ontology of finite Being describe nothing less than what all of us *always already* understand from our finite constitution, that is, understanding that being is the essence of finitude. Finitude depends on the fact that existence understands that being does not rest on the foundation of an essence "but uniquely *responds to* and *from* the there is of Being."[73] Nancy characterizes the birth of Being through its existence and event because it is something that happens: "Being happens, but it does not happen on itself and it does not reduce or return to itself—not without a remainder."[74] He goes on to specify that

what remains thus, or what is *coming* and does not stop coming as what remains, is what we call *existence*. It is "the existence of being," not in the sense of a predicate distinct from its essence, but in the sense of being that *is transitively* existence, or that *ex-ists*. Being exists the existent: it does not give the existent its sense *as* presupposition and end, but, rather, it is sense given with existence, as existence, more than a gift, being *toward* the world, where the world is not construed as a surrounding space, but as the multiple tracing out [*frayage*] of the singularity of existence.[75]

If existence is what comes and does not stop coming, hence a remains, it can do so only if it is based on a "there is [*il y a*] of something," that is, on Being. In this way, Being cannot be anything outside, before, or beyond its own *folding* of existence, because it is an existence that has no limit, no outside, but only the gift of itself. "Being *is*, in a transitive sense, ek-sisting."[76] But after having being deconstructed from all metaphysical categorizations, transcendentalisms, and idealizations, the ek-sisting Being "remains abandoned"[77] because it (the *abandoned Being*)[78] remains the sole predicament of Being. But why is it that what provokes meaning is the fact that there *is* being, that there *are* beings, and that *we* are as a community? This question finds an answer in Nancy's 1996 masterpiece *Being Singular Plural*.

The minimal ontological premise is that the meaning of Being is put into play as the "with" that is absolutely indisputable, because "Being is put into play among us; it does not have any other meaning except the dis-position of this 'between.'"[79] But how can this disposition become explicit in order to name the essence of Being? Nancy explains that Being is *singularly plural and plurally singular* not because it constitutes a particular predication of Being as if it had a certain number of attributes, but, on the contrary, the singular-plural constitutes the essence of Being because it is a constitution that automatically undoes every single, substantial essence of Being itself. Being singularly plural is an essence of Being that by being beyond any prior substance or preexistent existence remains only as "coessence." In other words, coessence, or being-with, designates the essence of the *cum*, the "co-" itself in the position of an essence. But this is not simply an addition. It operates in the same way as a collective power that is neither interior nor exterior to the members but rather consists in their collectivity.

But how can these three words—"Being," "singular," and "plural"— constitute the essence of Being if they have no determined syntax?[80] Since none of these three terms precedes or grounds the others, each designates the coessence of the others, and this same coessence puts essence itself in hyphenation, "being-singular-plural," which becomes a mark, explains Nancy, "of union and also a mark of division, a mark of sharing that effaces itself, leaving each term to its isolation *and* its being-with-the-others."[81] If, instead of beginning (as the metaphysical tradition was accustomed to) from the Being of being and proceeding to being itself with-one-another, one starts rather from being determined in its Being as being with-one-another, one will note that this, once again, is not a question of any supplementary property of Being but rather of the singular plural. The "singularity of each is indissociable from its being-with-many and *because*, in general, a singularity is indissociable from a plurality. . . . The concept of the singular implies its singularization and, therefore, its distinction from other singularities."[82] The singular is primarily "each one" and therefore also "with" and "among" all the others, just as the Latin term *singuli* indicates: the plural that designates the "one" that belongs to "one by one."

That Being is being-with, absolutely, this is what we must think. The *with* is the most basic feature of Being, the mark [*trait*] of the singular plurality of the origin or origins in it. Undoubtedly, the *with* as such is not presentable. . . . But if the unpresentability of "with" is not that of a hidden presence, then it is because "with" is the unpresentability of this pre-position, that is, the unpresentability of presentation itself. "With" does not add itself to Being, but rather creates the immanent and intrinsic condition of presentation in general. Presence is impossible except as copresence.[83]

Since Being gives itself as singular plural (because there is no appearing of oneself except as appearing to another), the "with," concludes Nancy, "is the fullest measure of (the) incommensurable meaning (of Being)."[84] Nancy believes that it is Heidegger's destruction that for the first time has put us on the right way (*chemin*) to reconfigure fundamental ontology, through an analysis that states how the being-with (*Mitsein, Miteinandersein, Mitdasein*) is essential to the constitution of Dasein itself. But Dasein is not a "man," a "subject," or an isolated and unique individual but rather "always the one, each one, with one another, *l'un-avec-l'autre*."[85] In *Being Singular Plural*, Nancy reminds us that throughout the whole history of philosophy, ontology occurred only at a speculative and abstract (metaphysical) level reserved for principles where "being-with" was subordinated to Being. But ontology, after deconstruction, as we have seen, primarily means a thinking of existence that is "globalness [*mondialité*] as such,"[86] that is, not according to an essence where Being could be presupposed and given to us as a meaning. "Being, explains Nancy, does not *have* meaning. Being itself, the phenomenon of Being, is meaning that is, in turn, its own circulation—and *we* are this circulation."[87] Dasein circulates in the community, sharing the meaning of Being, which cannot be anything else than the *being-with-one-another-in-the-world*.

In this condition, the remains of being in Nancy will depend on the fact that no *positing* of beings may be imposed on being and no sovereignty over beings may be attributed to being, because "sense does not add itself to being, does not supervene upon being, but is the opening of its very supervenience, of being-toward-the-world."[88] "In-the-world" refers to the realm in which Dasein is thrown, abandoned, offered, and set free together with the other Dasein that constitutes the community.[89] In this community of singular-plural Dasein, the world is *Mitsein*, a shared world, because Being, insofar as it is "in the world," is constitutively being-with and being-according-to-the-sharing. "The originary sharing of the world," explains Nancy, "is the sharing of Being, and the Being of the Dasein is nothing other than the Being of this sharing."[90] It is in this world, conceived as a "with," that the remains of Being find their place after metaphysics, because the world does not represent the exteriority of objects or a common substance that we all share but instead a sphere to work out Being anew, to put Being into play, hence "to be exposed together to ourselves as to heterogeneity, to the happening of ourselves."[91] From these analyses, Nancy concludes that "there is no ultimate language, but instead languages, words, voices, an originarily singular sharing of voices without which there would be no voice."[92] And it is this realization that provides an introduction for the remains of Being in the work of Gadamer, Tugendhat, and Vattimo.

§6. Gadamer's Conversations of Language

Like Nancy, Hans-Georg Gadamer also believes there is "no ultimate language" or "language of metaphysics," because language is not only "the house of Being," as Heidegger emphasized, but also *das Haus des Menschen*, "the house of the human being, a house where one lives, which one furnishes, and where one encounters oneself, or oneself in others."[93] For Gadamer, language is a "we" in which we are all assigned a place in relation to one another, but although this "place" is a community, as in

Nancy's thought, community for Gadamer "is living together in language, and language exists only in conversation."[94] Language is the "element in which we live, as fishes live in water . . . in linguistic interaction we call it a conversation."[95] Although Gadamer's well-known dictum states that "Being that can be understood is language,"[96] it is not "language" that the remains of Being in his philosophy will refer to but "conversation." If "Being that can be understood is language," then language might seem at first to be Being's remnant, but since "conversation is the medium in which language alone is alive,"[97] the remnant of Being is the conversation that takes place through language. Gadamer, like Schürmann, Derrida, and Nancy, also believes that the only reason the understanding of Being is possible at all is because there "is a 'there,' a clearing in being—i.e., a distinction between being and beings. Inquiry into the fundamental fact that this 'exists' is, in fact, inquiry into being."[98] This inquiry will always depend upon the condition that we all stand in the ontological difference and will never be able to overcome it. Gadamer specifies:

> What Being really means remains obscure, despite all the poems about the experience of one who was brought up in the thinking of the West and its religious horizon. What does "it is there" mean? This is the secret of the "Da," [there], not a secret of what is there, or that it is there. It does not mean the existence [Dasein] belonging to human beings, as in the term "struggle for existence," but rather it means that the "there" arises in the human being, and yet despite all its openness it remains at the same time hidden, concealed.[99]

Gadamer, by following Heidegger, who "modified the overcoming (Überwindung) of metaphysics and replaced it with a coming to terms with (*Verwindung*) metaphysics,"[100] was able to emphasize how philosophy can never totally and completely be cut loose from its historical heritage. Thus Gadamer believes "that there can never be 'philosophy' without metaphysics. And yet philosophy is perhaps only philosophy when it leaves metaphysical thinking and sentence logic behind it!"[101] Destruction was not meant to point back to a mysterious origin, an *arché*, or to repudiate this history but to "recover" from metaphysics in order to set thinking free, because the goal of destruction was only "to let the concept speak again in its interwovenness in living language" and had "nothing to do with obscure talk of origins and of the original."[102] Being is on the way to language because language's nature is conversational, and only through conversation can Being be understood, because it comes into language in conversation and not the other way around. If conversation is the essence of language, it goes also beyond Heidegger's analysis of Dasein's "very ownness" (*Jemeinigkeit*) and fallenness (*Verfallenheit*) into the world, because it "represents a more important experience: namely, conversation."[103]

Before venturing into the remains of Being in Gadamer, it is important to clarify the difference between the English terms "dialogue" and "conversation," as this will also introduce the remains. Although, literally, the German *Gespräch* should be translated as "discussion," *Dialog* as "dialogue," and *Unterhaltung* as "conversation," most translators of Gadamer's works have rightly translated *Gespräch* always as "conversation," not because of linguistic arbitrariness but because of a philosophical demand implicit in the meaning of *Gespräch*. When Gadamer refers to *Gespräch*, he is not alluding to something programmed, conducted, and organized in advance under the direction of a subject matter where the partners leave aside their particular points of view. On the contrary, a genuine *Gespräch* is never the one we wanted to conduct but rather the one we fall into and become involved in as it develops; we are led by it instead of being the leaders of it. In this way, the conclusion or truth reached by the *Gespräch* is actually produced through its own unprogrammed modalities, which we never have under control, and most of all this end is achieved without our knowing we would even reach it. Gadamer's *Gespräch* is closer to what in English we call "conversation," not "dialogue," which is a more specialized kind of conversation dedicated to finding the truth about something, as in the Platonic dialogues; in these dialogues, the interlocutors controlled the subject matter and the dialogue's outcome. To conduct a conversation instead means to allow oneself to be led by the subject matter, since what happens in a conversation is really without a goal. Since truth is not the main concern in a "conversation," we could speculate that if Gadamer had written in English he probably would have used "conversation" and not "dialogue" to refer to these open exchanges of the *Gespräch*, which are surrounded by positive tones of interchangeable views and not truth values.[104]

But why does Being, or any other word, exist only in conversation, that is, as the totality of a way of accounting by means of speaking and answering, but never in isolation? Gadamer brought the logic of conversation forward to go beyond linguistically fixed assertions that limited language to matters of fact, *Sachverhalte*. We need conversation, says Gadamer, because "our own concepts threaten to become rigid."[105] He explained in his magnum opus, *Truth and Method*, that even in the silent monotony of the Eleatic principle of being and *noein*, Greek thought followed the fundamental factualness of language; then, in overcoming the Eleatic conception of being, Plato saw the element of nonbeing in being as what really made it possible to speak of the existent at all.

> In the elaborate articulation of the logos of the *eidos*, the question of the real being of language could not be properly developed, since Greek thought was so full of the sense of the factualness of language. By pursuing the natural experience of the world in its linguistic form, it conceives the world as being. Whatever it conceives as existent emerges as *logos*, as an expressible matter of fact, from the surrounding whole that constitutes the world-horizon of language. What is thus conceived of as existing is not really the *object* of statements, but it "comes to language in statements." It thereby acquires its truths, its being evident in human thought. Thus Greek ontology is based on the factualness of language, in that it conceives the essence of language in terms of statements. [106]

Gadamer instead conceives the essence of language in terms of conversation, of live exchanges within the living community, because language's "human" origin means that man's being-in-the-world is primordially linguistic and, therefore, "whoever has language 'has' the world."[107] All human knowledge of the world has always had to be worked out again, because we do not live in it neutrally, separately, and independently but through what has been handed down to us. Heidegger's destruction enabled Gadamer to show that metaphysics conceived language as an element of Being itself rather than an activity of the subject. While Dasein's knowledge, through all classical and medieval philosophy, was incorporated in statements, language was not only left aside but also separated from thinking as something independent. Instead, language is inseparable from thinking, because, as Gadamer said, it is "the universal medium in which understanding occurs. . . . All understanding is interpretation, and all interpretation takes place in the medium of a language that allows the object to come into words."[108] Gadamer, through language, has shown how Being is never fully manifest, not only because each word leads to another constituting language but also because understanding never stands over against an "object": "understanding and interpretation are always intertwined with each other. Explication in language brings understanding to explicitness."[109]

What, then, is philosophy for Gadamer? Philosophy is a knowing that is quite "restricted and circumscribed by limits. This . . . is why we have hermeneutics—why we have a transcending of these limits. It's the same for Heidegger—we never know what Being is. It always seems to be a *topos*, an unattainable place that never becomes accessible."[110] The given is only the result of an interpretation, and the "given" itself cannot be separated from interpretation, because only within processes of interpretation is an observation expressible. An inevitable question arises at this point: does understanding come before interpretation, or is the reverse true? "Understanding," clarifies Gadamer, "is always already interpretation, and an interpretation is only a 'correct' interpretation if it emerges out of the performance of understanding."[111] As I explain in the introduction, hermeneutics is above all the art of understanding, and since understanding, by its very nature, is an occurrence in which history is operative, the task of hermeneutics for Gadamer is to demonstrate the "principle of effective history [*Wirkungsgeschichte*]." This principle is essential for our fundamental question of remnants, because it explains how the consciousness is always already affected by history and therefore "more Being than consciousness," as "it is not so much our judgments as it is our prejudices that constitute our Being."[112] We are so subject to history that even if all understanding is also an application, whenever we understand and interpret something, history affects Dasein's interpretative horizons in such a way that we cannot either clarify it or distance ourselves from it.

The German master of contemporary hermeneutical philosophy has explained, referring to Derrida's thought (on which he generously commented in several essays), that he took "conversation" as his starting point because "this is where the '*differance*' is realized—through conversation, in question and answer, the alterity of the true [*die Alterität des Wahren*] is brought to recognition."[113] Truth may emerge only from a conversation where the presentness of Being is dissolved in the question and answer and not based on it. Although conversations are always directed toward agreements, it is important to note that Gadamer is referring to an "agreement" not about content but rather about the maintenance of a common language of an endless conversation. This is why philosophizing "does not just start from zero but rather has to think further and speak further the language we speak."[114] Many have accused Gadamer's emphasis on language of "panlinguisticism," since his dictum seemed to mean that "Being," "understanding," and "language" were completely interwoven with one another, but he explained that he only meant to indicate that "Being speaks," in other words, that only through language can Being be understood. This formulation was indicated to Gadamer by Heidegger, who once explained to him that "*Die Sprache spricht*" ("language speaks"), and it speaks because when a person is speaking, he is also always restricted by language, and therefore one must "not think against language but with language."[115] The main point is not that everything is language but only that Being that can be understood, insofar as it can be understood, is language, because what cannot be understood poses an endless task of finding the right word. For these reasons, Gadamer believes that the real question of *Being and*

Time was not in what way Being can be understood but in what way understanding *is* Being, since the understanding of Being represents the existential particularity of Dasein.

According to Gadamer, this is the starting point of *Being and Time*—Dasein's understanding of itself in its Being—which leads thought to overcome traditional metaphysical self-consciousness, based on the presentness of presence considering itself as an object. Dasein, by understanding itself in its Being, instead is an understanding that always places itself in question, "which is not only grounded on the 'mine-ness' of my being that is revealed in the possibility of death, but at the same time encompasses all recognition of oneself in the other, which first opens up in conversation."[116] Gadamer, following Heidegger's destruction of the nature of metaphysics, whose question about the "whatness of beings" has obscured the question of the "there of Being," goes further, considering the notion of conversation as the most adequate mode of Being on the way to language, because it leaves behind the metaphysical subjectivity of the transcendental ego and especially the meaning-directed intention of the speaker. Now, if the "conversation" is all we have left, then we can conclude from Gadamer's analysis that conversation, thus Being, defines itself precisely "in what aims at being said beyond all words sought after or found,"[117] because "in a conversation, it is *something*, that comes to language, not one or the other speaker."[118] In this way, focusing on language, Gadamer has admitted that one can proceed in various ways, and he provides an introduction to my next section by saying that

The Anglo-Saxon tradition sought to work out the immanent logic of actually spoken language and in this way to challenge the artificial word-idols of traditional philosophical concept formation with a new analytic conscience. Here the work of Quine was very influential—and on the German scene the especially useful book by Ernst Tugendhat, *Traditional and Analytical Philosophy: Lectures on the Philosophy of Language*.[119]

§7. Tugendhat's Meanings of Sentences

Tugendhat's treatment of our question—how is it going with Being?—is outlined in the book he dedicated to Heidegger, *Traditional and Analytical Philosophy*,[120] and in essays such as "Language Analysis and the Critique of Ontology" and "The Question About Being and Its Foundation in Language." These titles immediately give an idea of the significance of language for Tugendhat because, as we will see, "the ontological question about being as being turns out to be a question about the understanding of sentences."[121] Tugendhat does not object to metaphysical philosophy because it orients itself toward objects through a prelinguistic relation and therefore conceives this relation in an overly simple fashion; rather, he finds the problem in that "it fails to take account of the fact that we refer linguistically to objects by means of expressions which—as singular terms—belong to a certain logical (formal-semantical) sentence-structure."[122]

Tugendhat, like Gadamer, believes that philosophy "is an activity which only becomes what it is in the process of being introduced,"[123] because it does not strive to explain something "that is not yet understood, but the clarification of what is already understood."[124] And what is already understood is Being, since all human understanding is grounded on an understanding of Being. Being happens in the "meaning of sentences" for Dasein because, in order to understand the meaning of a word, we do not need to see anything through a word. And even if there were something to see, it would be of no service in attaining intersubjective understanding. Tugendhat, like the other philosophers of the remains of Being, tried to find a way to eliminate a metaphysical mode of speaking about philosophy "from within," because he also believes that it is "the metaphor of seeing that dominates all traditional thinking, since this is the fundamental metaphor to which one can appeal in using any other metaphor."[125] For Tugendhat, philosophy is primarily ontology, a study of beings as such, but contrary to metaphysical ontology, the transfer of ontology to the sphere of language means that the problem of objects as such is actually investigated only when one questions how to refer to them linguistically. This transfer of ontology to the sphere of language takes us beyond the ontology of presence toward an analytical philosophy of language that "contains in itself the idea of a semantic ontology capable of taking on inherited ontology and transcendental philosophy."[126] If Being that can be understood is language, then analytical philosophy's goal is not to denounce the traditional philosophical problems as false, nor to clarify them through the explanation of their correspondence to expressive rules, but only to understand them better through what Tugendhat considers the natural successor of ontology: formal semantics.

> Traditional ontology itself points beyond to a new conception of the formal science, which, in the shape of a formal semantics, underlies all sciences. Formal semantics is, on the one hand, a language-analytical undertaking: it is semantics, it analyzes the meaning of linguistic expressions. On the other hand, it is formal,

in the sense that ontology was formal; and because it removes weaknesses of ontology, which are incapable of immanent resolution, it can lay claim to being ontology's legitimate successor.[127]

If Gadamer, through language, "works out" conversation, Tugendhat, also through language, works out "propositions," because "we never simply refer to objects, but always in such a way that we make predicative statements about them."[128] But contrary to Gadamer, Tugendhat brought forward a "semantization" of Heidegger's ontology that consisted in dissolving Being into the realm of semantics: statements, sentences, and propositions. "Dissolution," explains Tugendhat, "means that reflecting on objects gives birth to reflection on what is more than a pure object, and these are statements, or also the meaning of statements."[129] Tugendhat is convinced that there is no such thing as a reference to an object that is detached from a context of sentences, because the relation between language, or, better, linguistic signs, and reality depends upon the ontological function that sentences have for Dasein. Since linguistic signs are not representatives of other functions that would also be possible without them, that is, objects that signs would stand for, they represent the last ontological ground for knowledge. For Tugendhat, Being may only be given to us through linguistic usages that are not based, as in Gadamer, simply on "language" but rather on "linguistic signs" that are not mere signs but that "one understands and which many can understand in the same way."[130] This is why he specifies that "language does not mean anything; we have 'many' words and 'many' linguistic structures that we should understand."[131]

Metaphysics, for Tugendhat, has, from the beginnings of Greek philosophy up to Husserl, neglected language-analytical reflection and only operated within "a sensuous and even optical model"[132] because, as

Heidegger taught us, Being has always been interpreted as being-present-at-hand (*Vorhandenheit*). And this optical model is also guilty of the "nominalization" that Tugendhat identifies not only in the entire metaphysical tradition but also in Heidegger's insights, which Heidegger dissolved in order to translate into controllable statements. They had to be thus translated because, although Heidegger "went much farther than analytical philosophy," says Tugendhat, "his descriptive method lacked a criterion of verifiability."[133] Tugendhat, following Heidegger's destruction, has shown how, in the traditional ontological terminology, Being primarily has been captured in an objective or Platonic nominal perspective. He believes that it must now be reconsidered as a linguistic problem.

Even though the question of being appears to be the problem of the meaning of the word "is" in its different linguistic meanings (because "meanings do not exist in a Platonic heaven; they are meanings of sign"),[134] Heidegger talks as if all human understanding is based upon an understanding of Being. But if the meaning of Being is only found in linguistic signs, then it "appears to be that the understanding of a certain word—the word Being—somehow underlies all other understanding."[135] Tugendhat, examining Heidegger's "What Is Metaphysics?"[136] noticed that in this lecture the "understanding of Being" only occurs in conjunction with an understanding of "nothing." He also found that if the metaphysical tendency (which Heidegger shares with the tradition) to speak only in substantives is semanticized, a response to the question of whether Being only occurs in sentences is possible. Tugendhat's originality consists in replacing the talk of the "nothing" with the word "not," since the word Being, as we just noticed, only occurs in sentences. This replacement shows how Heidegger indirectly wanted to grasp the "extension of the word *is* in strict correlation with the use of the word *not....* Thus, according to his conception, it is the connection between affirmation and negation—the yes/no—that underlies the understanding of sentences."[137] Although it is this connection between the words "yes" and "no" that confirms that the ontological question about being as Being depends on the understanding of sentences, it must still be explained why Being is only found in the "meanings of sentences." Language is not a simple medium between us and the reality of objects, because in its semantical dimension there are some determinations that do not depend on mere objectivity but contribute to their own understanding. Tugendhat demonstrates this through the general function of the predicate.

If the predicate must stand for something, and if this something must be capable of being represented, it cannot be a matter of sensory intuition, because we would have to represent something that corresponds to the entire scope of the predicate, that is, corresponds also to nonsensible representations. While Plato and Aristotle tried to call this nonsensible representation "*noein*," and Husserl, through the eidetic abstraction, tried to give a foundation to the existence of intuitions of such essences, Tugendhat instead explained:

> We do not need such a representation to understand the understanding of predicates. We explain to someone the meaning of a predicate (and thereby reconstrue our own understanding) not by pointing to a general essence but by applying the predicate to different objects, whereby we explain the extent of its classificatory function, and by refusing its application to other objects, whereby we explain the extent of its discriminatory function. Understanding the meaning of the predicate does not consist in seeing some-

thing but in mastering the rule which determines the application of the predicate. The generality of the predicate is a rule-generality, not a "general object."[138]

Tugendhat is suspicious as to whether the predicate, in a sentence such as "the sky is blue," also stands for something, in this case the "blueness" of the sky. Although blueness is indeed something that may be designated as a being, Tugendhat notices that in moving from "the sky is blue" to "the blueness of the sky," a change occurs in the form of the expression: "the predicate 'is blue' has been changed by a so-called nominalization into the singular term 'the blueness.'"[139] What is expressed in the verbal sentence as an essence of the object is, in the nominal sentence, set off by itself as a real content and established as a condition or state. But with this change (nominalization), the nominalized form (the blueness, that is, an abstract object) is still semantically secondary relative to the predicative form (is blue), because "we do not *represent* objects to ourselves, we *mean* objects."[140]

What makes the expression "Being" so difficult, according to him, is its connection with the ambiguous verbal expression "is," because we may either employ it as a singular term,[141] or as a pronoun and without a supplementing predicative expression (as in the sentence "John is"), or as the so-called copula in a predicate sentence (as in "the sky is blue"). The problem lies in the fact that when one speaks of "a being," only the use of "is," in the sense of "exists," is involved, since "a being" means "something that is": when the word "is" is used without a supplementing predicative expression, the substantival expression "being" is univocal and has the same sense of "existent." All traditional metaphysical philosophers were oriented toward the copulative "is," because they understood it as the "is" of a "being." Aristotle, for example, took "being" to be that for which the predicate stands, in other words, the being-thus-and-so (*Das So-seiend-Sein*) of the object.

Since our understanding constantly transcends its articulation in sentences, we must now ask: what is the dimension through which we pass from sentence to sentence? According to Tugendhat, it is not possible to answer this question because every naming of entities, objects, or sentences remains within language, which is always embedded in sentences. Note that Tugendhat reaches the meaning of sentences as the only indication of Being's remains after Heidegger's destruction not by questioning what "language means in Being" but by asking what "Being means in language," because the "universal dimension in which we live with understanding is not primarily a world of objects, entities, of facts, but a world of sentences, of unities of meaning."[142]

§8. Vattimo's Events of Weakness

More so than in Schürmann, Derrida, Nancy, Gadamer, and Tugendhat, of all the evidence for the remains of Being that I have outlined in this book, Vattimo's work is probably the one that best responds to Heidegger's call to "work out Being for itself anew" and "grasp its last remnant of a possession," because, as I explained in the introduction, Vattimo is the architect of this ontology of remnants. What I call the "ontology of remnants" he named the "ontology of actuality," and its fundamental question for him is also very similar to ours: "ontology of actuality is used here," he explained in *Nihilism and Emancipation*, "to mean a discourse that attempts to clarify what Being signifies in the present situation."[143] His answer to this question is the "event of weakness,"[144] which also finds a productive space in our question, "How is it going with Being?" The answer Vattimo gives is this: if Being has been able to endure so long, it is not "because of its force . . . but because of its weakness."[145] I am treating the remains of being in Vattimo last because his is an indirect fusion of the other five systems of remains (since Vattimo is the only one who has commented on all of them and therefore appropriated some of their ideas) and because he provides a useful way to introduce the next part of my study.

According to this Italian philosopher, we have not been able to answer the fundamental question of philosophy—why *is* Being, and why *is* there not rather nothing?—because "Being lacks a reason": there is no reason sufficient to explain why Being is. This implies the weakness of Being, because "if Being had a strong reason to be," explains Vattimo, "then metaphysics would have significance, would have strength. But as things are, Being . . . is historical and casual, happened and happening."[146] For these reasons, Vattimo believes that philosophy is weak thought, an ontology of weakness, and thus philosophical effort ought to focus on interpretation as a process of weakening the objective weight of the presence of Being.

Vattimo has taken literally Heidegger's indication that the new epoch of Being, after the destruction of metaphysics, would not depend on our decisions but rather on recognizing how we belong to this same destruction, that is, to "a philosophy of 'decline,' a philosophy which sees what is constitutive of Being not as the fact of its prevailing, but of the fact of its disappearing."[147] Putting Heidegger's *Verwindung* of metaphysics at the heart of his philosophical position, Vattimo's remnant of Being is the "event of weakness," which, as we will see, is the most radical development of this ontology of remnants, because it fuses Schürmann's emphasis on the "event" and Gadamer's insistence on "language" in such a way that it allows Vattimo to consider Tugendhat's identification of Being and language as valid—although not enough, as he explains:

> In Tugendhat, the Heideggerian identification of Being and language is valid. And precisely by seeking to avoid the "relativistic" outcome of this identification, one may also discover the other "identification" in Heidegger, that of Being with the event. Truth is only because and so long as Dasein is, but Dasein is historical and eventual and experiences truth only in the sphere of a historical horizon in which only every specific sentence gains sense.[148]

Instead of Being and language, Vattimo couples Being and event, but in such a way that Being's "eventual" nature will depend on the linguistic horizon that constitutes it. The term "*Ereignis*" (event), used by Heidegger to indicate (not define) Being in *Contributions to Philosophy*, was meant to mark, according to Vattimo, the new ontological approach that excludes all essentialist views of Being. Vattimo's starting point is not only the end of metaphysics but the end of deconstruction: "what is ahead of philosophy as its goal, after deconstructionism, is a labor of stitching things back together, of reassembly."[149] In this condition, Being becomes an event, because philosophy no longer corresponds to the Platonic agenda of understanding Being through the Eternal but rather seeks to do so through its own history; that is, it redirects itself toward history. But this is only possible if Being and event are fused together. Such a Being would derive not from Being "as it is" but from Being viewed as the product of a history of formulations, interpretations, and deconstructions that "are 'givens' of destiny understood as a process of trans-mission. They are points of reference we keep encountering each time we engage in thinking here and now."[150] If Being for Vattimo consists in a trans-mission, in the forwarding and destiny (*Ueber-lieferung* and *Ge-schick*) of a series of echoes, linguistic resonances, and messages coming from the past and from others in the form of events, what is the philosophical position that responds to this process of the weakening of Being?

Hermeneutics is the philosophical position that grasps Being's vocation of giving itself as the truth of human language, and therefore it presents itself as the most appropriate to the "thinking that corresponds to Being as *event*."[151] The "eventual" nature of Being is nothing but "the disclosure of historico-linguistic horizons within which beings (things, men, etc.) come into presence."[152] In this way, Being never really *is* but sends itself, is on the way, transmits itself. Having said this, one might think that language is something bigger or prior to Being; on the contrary, it is an event of Being itself. For Vattimo, this "eventuality" indicates that everything we see as a structure, essence, or theorem (such as the idea of truth as the conformity of the proposition to the thing) is an event, an historical aperture or disclosure of Being. Being presupposes this disclosure, which is not an object of philosophical research but rather that into which it is always already thrown.

The key teaching of Heidegger, according to Vattimo, is his idea of the ontological difference: the difference between being and beings. Although it is just on the forgetfulness of this difference that metaphysical thought was able to evolve into a strong thought, the destruction of metaphysics has not only produced a "weak thought" but has also dissolved Being into its own "becoming" interpretations. Being is not what endures, what is and cannot not be—as Parmenides, Plato, and Aristotle would have it—but only what becomes because it "becomes" from the ontological difference. What becomes comes to life and dies and for that reason has a history, a permanence of its own in its concatenated multiplicity of meanings and interpretations. After having found Being's "becoming," thus its event, in the ontological difference, Vattimo goes on to specify that whereas "Being is not identifiable with beings, with the particular entities given to us in our experience (things, facts, persons)," it is "comparable to the light by which entities become visible."[153] This light can also be understood as the linguistic horizon in which we are surrounded, because beings become visible to us only within a horizon that is historically determined, as it is impossible to attribute to it the immutable objectivity of the "objects" that appear within it. The "difference" of the ontological difference indicates that we can only truly distinguish Being from beings when we conceive "it as historical-cultural happenings, as the instituting and transforming of those horizons in which entities time and again become accessible to man."[154] But how do they become accessible? Through language: all experience of the world is primarily a series of linguistic events that happen to Dasein as the being that is "in-the-world."

Being-in-the-world does not mean being effectively in contact with all things that constitute the world but rather being always already (*immer schon*) familiar with a totality of meanings, that is, with a context of references, projects, or, as Heidegger says, tools. If Dasein exists and is in-the-world as a thrown project (*geworfener Entwurf*), then our existence would also always already be thrown into language, because Dasein exists in the form of a project in which things are only insofar as they belong to this project. And since this occurs only in the form of meanings, things become accessible because every act of knowledge is nothing more than an interpretation of this existence in-the-world, making the universal structure of knowledge interpretative: "to know" is always "to interpret." This hermeneutic structure of existence helps Vattimo explain why "hermeneutics itself *is a form of the dissolution of*

Being in the era of an accomplished metaphysics."[155] In this context, the world of ontology becomes the world of active nihilism, where Being has an opportunity to reoccur in an authentic form only through its own weakening. As soon as Western philosophy realizes this, "it becomes nihilistic," says Vattimo; "it acknowledges that its own argumentative process is always historically and culturally situated."[156]

Active nihilism is the vocation and nature of hermeneutics, according to Vattimo, because "Being, whose meaning we seek to recuperate, tends to identify itself with nothingness, with the fleeting traits of an existence enclosed between the boundaries of birth and death."[157] In other words, Being as the "event of weakness" is a extension of Heidegger's interpretation of Nietzsche's nihilism. As the discovery that alleged that values, truths, lies, and metaphysical structures are just a play of forces, nihilism became, thanks to Nietzsche, the revelation of the will to power as that which dislocates and subverts prevailing hierarchical relations. In this condition, man was founded by rolling "from the center towards X" and Being as "nothingness." As we know, Heidegger commented on Nietzsche's nihilism as the process in which, at the end, "there is nothing to Being as such" and coined "*Andenken*" to refer to the thought that "lets go of Being as foundation" after metaphysics. For Vattimo, the outcome of thinking about nihilism and *Andenken*, and thus of Nietzsche and Heidegger, ought to be hermeneutical thought understood "as the effort to constitute the drift of that which is present on the basis of its connections with past and future."[158]

Although Vattimo recognizes that hermeneutics originally was a theory that legitimized its interpretations by demonstrating it could be a correct interpretation of a message *from the past* by reconstructing the history of a certain number of events, he is more interested in indicating how it can also be an interpretation *from within*, that is, from what it always already belongs to, "since this belonging is the very condition for the possibility of receiving messages."[159] But this belonging is nothing else than the remains of Being, or in Vattimo's words, the events of Being. Hermeneutic philosophy becomes the key for the future because interpretation is, in itself, a response to a message, an articulated response to its own belonging, tradition, and history from which it arises—because we always know, at least to a certain extent, where we are going. Because hermeneutics, then, is a theory that tries to grasp the meaning of the remains of Being that have been transmitted as a consequence of the destruction of metaphysics, I end this chapter with a passage from Vattimo's magnum opus, *Beyond Interpretation*, that will introduce the next chapter and prepare the way for the consequences of the remains of Being, the investigation of the "generation" of philosophy.

> In contrast to the metaphysical historicism of the nineteenth century (Hegel, Comte, Marx), hermeneutics does not take the meaning of history to be a "fact" that must be recognized, cultivated, and accepted . . . ; the guiding thread of history appears, is given, only in an act of interpretation that is confirmed in dialogue with other possible interpretations and that, in the final analysis, leads to a modification of the actual situation in a way that makes the interpretation "true." . . . The novelty and the importance of hermeneutics ultimately consists in the affirmation that the rational (argumentative) interpretation of history is not "scientific" in the positivistic sense and yet neither is it purely "aesthetic." The task of contemporary hermeneutics seems to be that of articulating in an ever more complete and explicit form this original inspiration; which means furthermore the task of corresponding responsibly to the appeal arising from its inheritance.[160]

3. GENERATING BEING THROUGH INTERPRETATION

THE HERMENEUTIC ONTOLOGY OF REMNANTS

WHAT HERMENEUTICS IS REALLY MEANT TO ACHIEVE IS NOT MERELY TAKING COGNIZANCE OF SOMETHING AND HAVING KNOWLEDGE ABOUT IT, BUT RATHER AN EXISTENTIAL KNOWING, I.E., A BEING [*EIN SEIN*]. IT SPEAKS FROM OUT OF INTERPRETATION AND FOR THE SAKE OF IT. . . . AS FAR AS I AM CONCERNED, IF THIS PERSONAL COMMENT IS PERMITTED, I THINK THAT HERMENEUTICS IS NOT PHILOSOPHY AT ALL, BUT IN FACT SOMETHING PRELIMINARY WHICH RUNS IN ADVANCE OF IT AND HAS ITS OWN REASONS FOR BEING: WHAT IS AT ISSUE IN IT, WHAT IT ALL COMES TO, IS NOT TO BECOME FINISHED WITH IT AS QUICKLY AS POSSIBLE, BUT RATHER TO HOLD OUT IN IT AS LONG AS POSSIBLE. . . . IT WISHES ONLY TO PLACE AN OBJECT WHICH HAS FALLEN INTO FORGETFULNESS BEFORE TODAY'S PHILOSOPHERS FOR THEIR "WELL-DISPOSED CONSIDERATION."

—MARTIN HEIDEGGER, *ONTOLOGY: THE HERMENEUTICS OF FACTICITY* (1923)

IN THIS LAST CHAPTER, I AM GOING TO TRY NOT ONLY TO explain where philosophy goes from this ontology of remnants or philosophy of remains but also to give a function to this same ontology through its logic. In other words, I am going to show how hermeneutics is the philosophy of generation, that is, that which generates Being. But how can it generate Being if, as I said, "*to on*," "*es gibt Sein*," and "*il y a de l'être*" always already? In order to answer this question, we need to further specify the hermeneutic ontology that has been guiding our path because, as Heidegger explains in the epigraph to this chapter, hermeneutics is in advance of philosophy. Hermeneutics is not in advance or beyond philosophy because it is capable of solving questions that philosophy cannot but, rather, for being able to hold them as long as possible.

If Dasein's ontological priority over other entities, as I described in chapter 1, depended on its possibility of existence, and if interpretation was primarily the uncovering of the basic (existential) structures of Dasein, then hermeneutics is "philosophically primary," because it sets out from the interpretation of Dasein. As Heidegger says, hermeneutics is not meant to achieve a cognizance of something in order to have "knowledge about it, but rather an existential knowing, i.e., a Being."[1] Philosophy sets out from the hermeneutics of Dasein because all philosophical questioning arises from existence and also always returns to it. In the seminar on Heraclitus's fragments (a seminar conducted with Eugen Fink in the winter semester of 1966–1967 at the University of Freiburg), Heidegger clarified further what he meant, by using Wittgenstein's example of the difficulty of the thought of Being in relation to a man in a room from which he wants to get out: first, the man attempts to get out from the room through a window that is too high for him, then a chimney that is too narrow, but if he "simply turned around, he would see that the door was open all along. We ourselves," continues Heidegger, "are permanently set in motion and caught in the hermeneutical circle."[2]

Hermeneutics involves a circle; that is, it presupposes that we cannot understand a part without some understanding of the whole or understand the whole without some understanding of its parts, because to learn what being is we need to examine Dasein's Being. This is why understanding the distinction between existence and reality (the ontological difference) means understanding Being as the horizon of that distinction. But whence does this circle come? Heidegger suggests in *Being and Time* that the circle in understanding stems from Dasein's inherent circularity, that since it is in-the-world, its being is at issue. Heidegger agrees with Wittgenstein on the difficulty of thinking, because he also recognizes how philosophy has focused for too long on the "well-disposed considerations," forgetting that Being, just as the door, was simply available all along. For Heidegger, it is not only necessary to know that we are permanently set in motion and caught in this hermeneutic circle, that is, to stay in it "in the right way"; it is also necessary to work out Being anew from within. Interpreting the destruction of metaphysics as the moment in history where we may begin to think the remains of Being—since we cannot overcome metaphysics but only appropriate it, come to terms with it, or attempt to grasp its last resonance (as we did in chapter 2)—implies that Being remains and that it cannot be set apart.

Being can only be generated through interpretation, because Being is already there; it is something that keeps remaining and that Dasein must hold as long as possible. Just as the interpretations of a piece of music emanate from the work of art itself, as Gadamer explained, our interpretations of Being emanate from Being's "is," its "gratuity" or "happening," into which we were thrown well before we even attempted to grasp it in an ontology. This is why philosophy, guided by the question about Being, had to destroy the content of this traditional ontology down to the original experiences in which the first guiding determinations of Being were acquired, in order to reveal new possibilities and directions that had been obscured. As Heidegger explains, these new possibilities hold "the unborn generation beyond the deceased, and saves it for the coming rebirth of mankind out of the originary."[3]

Although it is only through interpretation after the end of metaphysics that Being is newly generated, this same generation (always in the form of remnants) only occurs within metaphysics, hence, as the remains of Being, because, as we have seen, metaphysics can only be overcome through incorporation, that is, hermeneutics. Such a theory has its origin not only in Heidegger, Gadamer, Derrida, Dilthey, and Schlei-ermacher but also extends as far back as Greek philosophy in Plato's *Symposium*, where Socrates tells the truth of love by giving an account of the advice of Diotima that he had heard years before. Socrates, in-stead of speaking of his reception of the teachings of Diotima, of acquir-ing or possessing his knowledge, refers to initiation and appropriation. That is, truth, Being, or things in general do not make their way from the past by means of cultural transmission but by a kind of "translation that is appropriative rather than cognate with an original."[4] The peculiarity of this appropriation is that it resists objectifications and renderings in order to recuperate what was lost—not as an object, an apophantic en-tity, but rather as that which remains. As Gerald L. Bruns points out,[5] such a theory of generation can be found in this passage from Plato's *Symposium*:

> Mortal nature [Diotima says] always seeks as much as it can to exist forever and to achieve immortality. But it is able to do this only by means of generation [*genesei*], its way of always leaving be-hind another, young one against old age. It is particularly in this that each living individual is said to be alive and to be itself—just as one is described as oneself and the same person from childhood until becoming old. But in actuality one hasn't any characteristics at all whereby one can be called the same person. One is always becoming a new person, losing things, portions of hair, flesh, bones, blood, and all the stuff of the body. And not only the body. In the soul as well one's habits and character, beliefs, desires, plea-sures, pains, fears—none of these things remain the same in any-one—they arise and die out. But what's even stranger than these facts is that we not only gain knowledge and lose it, so that we

don't remain the same people with respect to what we know, but that every single example of knowledge suffers the same thing. For a man is said to study when there is a departing of knowledge, and study, by implanting new knowledge in place of what has left, saves the memory of it, so that it seems like the same thing. It is in this way that everything mortal is preserved—not by its being utterly the same forever, like the divine, but by what is old and withdrawing leaving behind something else, something new like itself. It is by this method, Socrates, that the mortal partakes of immortality, she explained, in the body and in all other respects.[6]

Although this passage does not refer directly to Being, note that it brings forward a theory of generation whose logic legitimizes my ontology of remnants. Things remain by means of generation; in other words, although Being is not the same eternally, it is always becoming through its own remnants or, as Plato puts it, "by what is old and withdrawing leaving behind something else, something new like itself." This is a hermeneutical process because, as we have seen in the introduction, *hermeneuein* is that exposition that not only brings tidings, with respect to "preserving a message," but, most of all, brings "together what is concealed within the old." In this way, it generates from what is concealed within the old "becoming," through its own remnants, or, better, generating through its own generations. This is why *not what is but what remains is essential for philosophy.*

Being has taken leave of its metaphysical configurations not simply by revealing its nature as contingent or falsely foundational but also by giving itself in the form of that which "is not" but has always already been, that which holds sway only as a remnant, in a faded and weakened form. To this destiny of the weakening of Being belongs, according to

Vattimo, the nexus between the event of Being and human mortality: "the historico-destination clearings in which things come to Being are epochal and not 'eternal,' simply because the generations or 'Daseins' through which and for which they come to light, are not eternal."[7] Nor are they eternal for Derrida, who considered that the activity connoted by the *a* in *différance* referred "to the generative movement in the play of differences [that] are neither fallen from the sky nor inscribed once and for all in a closed system."[8] The logics of remnants I am about to analyze will be neither eternal nor inscribed in a closed system, as most logics tried to be, but rather anarchic (in Schürmann's sense) and historic (in Vattimo's sense).

§9. Logics of Discursive Continuities

While Dasein is permanently caught in the hermeneutic circle holding the remains of Being, ontology, as I said, now depends not on Being but on Being's remnants, on the remains of Being. These remains may only be grasped through interpretation, because productive interpretations, in addition to appropriating Being, also "generate Being."[9] The ontological meaning of the term "generation" (or "generational") depends on offspring that are descended from a common ancestor (Being). In order to introduce the logical function of generation, that is, the logics of discursive continuities, it is important to read this passage, where Vattimo specifies the role of productive interpretation for the first time:

> What does a productive interpretation generate? It generates Being, new senses of experience, new ways for the world to announce itself, which are not only other than the ones announced

"before." Rather, they join the latter in a sort of *discursus* whose logic (also in the sense of Logos) consists precisely in the continuity. . . . Ontological hermeneutics replaces the metaphysics of presence with a concept of Being that is essentially constituted by the feature of dissolution. Being gives itself not once and for all as a simple presence; rather, it occurs as announcement and grows into the interpretations that listen and correspond (to Being).[10]

An ontology of remnants has its own logic, which, as Vattimo suggests, consists of a discursive continuity that, since it is "generated from the dissolution of the metaphysics of presence,"[11] does not have any objective status but only "remaining" statutes, that is, regulations that emanate from within. Now, it is essential to note that "remaining" is not only the present participle of "remain" (from old French *remaindre*, to remain) but, most of all, the simple verb of "remain." "Remaining," through its verbal function, denotes the state or action of a remain that, for us, is nothing other than Being's remnant. Thus, when I was questioning the remains of Being, I was actually seeking the moving verb within it, that is, its discursive continuity. This discursive continuity is "generational," because in its act of bringing into Being it reproduces and produces Being. It produces Being because productive interpretations generate Being, and it reproduces Being because it is also a "remainder" of Being. A remainder is what remains in favor of one other than the grantor and follows upon the natural termination of a prior intervening possessor; in other words, it is what takes effect in favor of an unidentifiable person (as one not yet born) or upon the "occurrence" of an uncertain event that is not presentable because it is the condition of such presentations and escapes all forms of apprehension. It is also important to emphasize that this hermeneutical ontology of the logic of remains is bound up with our fundamental question—how is it going with Being?—because the fact that Being is nothing apart from its own remains implies a logic capable of being discursive and continuous, that is, of appropriating Being's remains.

This logic of discursive continuities is, as I said, an-archic and historic because it goes beyond the traditional meaning of "logics" as the study of criteria for the evaluation of arguments. It is a logic in the basic Greek sense of *logos* (traced back by Heidegger from Aristotle's understanding of life and praxis in his *Seminar on Heraclitus* and *Phenomenological Interpretations of Aristotle: Initiation Into Phenomenological Research*), hence of "making manifest." While in the traditional meaning logic ultimately comes to decide what may or may not be, the second, Greek sense is based upon an experience of speech, *rede*, as the basic trait of human cognition in order to make being manifest. Although Heidegger explains this in order to overcome the metaphysical idea according to which the supreme form of knowledge for Aristotle was contained in the simple apprehension of *nous*, he also gives a justification for my characterization of this logic as an-archic and historic, because this same "speech" is based upon the concept of *kinesis*, that is, change. *Kinesis* is an ontological movement of disclosure that is bound up with the ontological movement of Dasein, which is not only finite but also *kinetic*, that is, in motion. In *Pathmarks*, Heidegger explains, using the famous example of the production of a chair, the connection is between generation and this ontological movement:

> Take the case of generation: a table coming into existence. Here we obviously find movements. But Aristotle does not mean "movements" performed by the carpenter in handling the tools and the wood. Rather, in the generation of the table, Aristotle is

thinking precisely *of the movement of what is being generated itself and as such.* The change of something into something, such that in the change the very act of change itself breaks out into the open, i.e., comes into appearance along with the changing thing.[12]

Although I will analyze the problem of generation in the next section, note that the movement of what is generated and the generated thing are not infinite movements but rather movements from within the same being. The carpenter's movement is nothing other than Dasein's finite movement as opposed to the infinite apprehension of presence or *nous*. Dasein, living in finite possibilities, aware of its own possibility, precedes actuality in order to understand and produce a shift from the priority of the eternal to the priority of the finite. Now, since logic (in the *logos* sense) "is the phenomenon that is supposed to clarify what being means,"[13] and Being is nothing other than its own remains, it is just through the experience of speech that the moving verb within the remaining Being can be clarified and kept. This logic is discursive, because it must converse with its tradition, and it is continuous, because this same conversation with its own tradition must not be interrupted but occurs continually.

The an-archism and historicism I mentioned above, in contrast to the eternal and closed systems of most logics, also depends on recourse to the original Greek meaning of logic, because while Heidegger was preserving the Greeks' own practical wisdom, he also recalled that the issue of logic, understood more originally, is not only a "doing" but at the same time a "letting." The an-archism of logic that I refer to is hidden in the same *kinesis*, which indicates, as Schürmann pointed out, a "doing" or an "action," because "originally knowledge is thus something to be gained, conquered by the 'logical' measure over hubris, the lack of measure."[14] This conquering of the lack of measure implies not only that previous lack upon which it operated but also an an-archic action that allows a disposition that is "logical in the original sense."[15] Together with the an-archic action required by this logic, it is essential to emphasize its "letting" or "appropriating" nature—that is, its historicism. Regarding the necessary historicism of such logic, Vattimo explains:

> The very logic with which discourse proceeds (for it does have one—and not an arbitrary one) is inscribed within a situation composed of controlling procedures given the time and again in the same *non-pure* mode in which historical and cultural conditions of experience are given. Perhaps the model to keep in mind—which is in fact always already operative in philosophical procedures—is that of literary and art criticism: all critical discourse and evaluation unfolds on the basis of a set of canons historically constituted by the history of art and taste.[16]

As it is discursive and continuous, the logic of remains must be capable of making its intrinsic "generational" procedure function. This procedure, as I said, consists in its *production* (an-archic) and *reproduction* (historic) of Being. The logic of remains reproduces Being because "Being" still counts as a used-up term. It is our duty to grasp its last resonance as a possession and a production because this "possession" is nothing other than the remains of Being, which inevitably offers itself for thought (before or beyond Being), "affecting" further remains. This is the logic that functioned through of all six remnants I worked through in chapter 2, since they are all "generational." Each of them was a reproduction and production of Being beyond metaphysics. For example, Schürmann's traits indicated the systemic features that connect epochs in order to give shape to new modalities of coming events, and Derrida's traces belong, as a simulacrum of a presence, to metaphysics, and at the same time they unfold their own effects for further residues. Nancy's copresence, instead, was a mark that shared itself continually with the past and future, just as Gadamer's conversations allow themselves to be conducted from a previous subject matter in order to pursue interpretation without knowing where it will end. And while Tugendhat's sentences were formed from linguistic signs that constitute the same material that made new meaningful formations of sentences, Vattimo's events are constituted from the linguistic horizon that constitutes them in order to form further transmissions of itself.

The discursive continuity of this logic, as I noted, does not have any objective status but only remaining statutes. Etymologically, the Latin term *statutum*, law or regulation, comes from *statutus*, the past participle of *statuere*, to set up, station, and from *status*, position, state. All remains of Being share the same internal regulation, station, or position characteristic of Heidegger's worn-out Being: indeterminability, unpresentability, and ungraspability. They do not presence or represent anything objectual except their own remnants, which, although they are not presentable (or objective), are the condition of such presentations and escape all forms of prehension. These remains constitute the horizon or realm within which every entity gives itself as something and through it appears and disappears. Schürmann's traits did not represent anything except the so-called economic mutation that gave shape to the event of Being, while Derrida, in order to name the trace, which is always displacing itself and without site, had to come up with the *différance* that marks its movement. Neither do Nancy's copresences nor Gadamer's conversations represent anything. They are the names given to the unattainable place that never becomes accessible through presence. Although Tugendhat's sentences could be meant to represent their own meaning (redness for the red castle), they always give birth to what is more than a pure object, just as Vattimo's events become visible to us only within horizons that can be historically, linguistically, or even culturally determined.

The remaining (productive and reproductive) statutes of this logic belong also to the historical, finite, thrown constitution of Dasein, because, as I said, the logics of discursive continuities do not function in order to have an infinite apprehension of presence but only to make Being manifest, in other words, to "make it remain." Although Dasein is historical as long as it is truly "*Da*," "there," it distinguishes itself from beings-in-the-world because it is an existence of continuous discourses. But this distinction from ontic beings is valid insofar as it constitutes itself as a historical totality that goes along continuously and historically among the various possibilities that make up its own existence, which may either be authentic or inauthentic. Although the historical authenticity of Dasein is dependent insofar as it can explicitly anticipate its own death, it must be true also in another, more profound "generational" sense, that is, have "at its disposal determined and qualified possibilities and [having] relationships to past and future generations precisely because it is born and dies in the literal, biological sense of the words."[17] This relationship to past and future generations (just as the an-archic production and historic reproduction of Being) constitutes the remaining statutes of this logic in such a way that is not something "reached" but rather "delineated by itself." It is delineated by itself because it is Being that throws it, not Dasein. As a thrown project, Dasein is not the "one who throws" but, as I explained in chapter 1, the "one thrown." The horizons within which entities, including Dasein as the thrown project, appear have "roots in the past and are open towards the future, that is to say, they are historical-finite horizons."[18] Since it is Being that is "preventing all 'goals' and breakdown of every explainability,"[19] Dasein cannot consider itself the master of Being but only the one who experiences itself as projected by Being itself. It is in this condition that Heidegger proposed his hermeneutics of Dasein, his philosophy of finitude that *generated* around the concept of interpretation and, most of all, "from within."

§10. Generating Being "from Within"

At the end of all ontologies it is always asked: Where do we go from here? How is such an ontology to be applied? Is this a foundational ontology? These are all practical-metaphysical questions that forget that ontology's task is only to hold on to Being as long as possible because in philosophy, just "as in democracy, one should fight within the ongoing movement, from the inside, to turn it in other directions."[20] These other directions are not different subject matters but further understandings of Being, that is, further remnants of Being, like the ones I have worked out anew through Schürmann, Derrida, Nancy, Gadamer, Tugendhat, and Vattimo. These philosophers have indicated other directions that have generated, following the logic of discursive continuities, different remnants that, as Wittgenstein's conception of "family resemblance" indicates, share a lack of boundaries and exhibit the distances between them. Since metaphysics, as I explain in the introduction, cannot be overcome but only gotten over from within, hermeneutics becomes the only adequate way to think Being within its own history and modalities, as it (Being) requires. Hermeneutics is the philosophy of generations, that is, the most suitable for generating Being from within, as Being demands, because it is also a knowledge less of what Being means in itself than of how we stand with respect to it. Since Dasein moves within horizons where it is not possible to determine Being as such, once and for all, or in a way that a change in its perspective will not require us to revise it, then there can be no such thing as understanding that is not also interpretation. Rather, everything is interpretable to the point that "to know is to interpret, [and] to interpret is also to produce new history,"[21] because "much remains for us to think but little for us to know,"[22] as Vattimo and Schürmann taught us.

Ontology does not depend any longer on its destruction by metaphysics but only on its remnants, which follow the logic of discursive continuities, where the remaining statutes are also always already "ongoing" statutes of Being; in other words, they generate further Being through its verbal (kinetic) function. The verb that is inside the remains of Being reproduces and produces Being through interpretation because it denotes the state and action of the remains: that which emanates from within. The destruction of Being as presence essentially belonged to "the formulation of the question of Being and [was] possible exclusively within such a formulation,"[23] but the new question was also conceived from within the fundamental question: Heidegger considered it "the hearth-fire that glows in the asking of the fundamental question."[24]

Being requires such treatment because we are in a situation, as I explained, where principally there is Being: Being is in the "driver's seat" and is given to us without our request, decision, or control, in the form of remains. But in order to understand the generation of Being from within, it is first necessary to show how such "gratuity" or "givenness" is not constitutive only of Being but also of Being's remains. What models or examples are there from the history of philosophy of things so ontologically constituted as "remaining" so as to require and invite us to consider not what they are but what remains of them? Gadamer and Luther, through their understanding of the "classical" and the biblical Scriptures, have indirectly given us the closest model there is to Being's remnant. In this famous passage, Gadamer explains the power of the "classical" and also indirectly provides us with a model of Being's remains.

> The classical is fundamentally something quite different from a descriptive concept used by an objectivizing historical consciousness. It is a historical reality to which historical consciousness belongs and is subordinate. The "classical" is something raised above the vicissitudes of changing times and changing tastes. It is immediately accessible, not through that shock of recognition, as it were, that sometimes characterizes a work of art for its contemporaries and in which the beholder experiences a fulfilled apprehension of meaning that surpasses all conscious expectations. Rather, when we call something classical, there is a consciousness of something enduring, of significance that cannot be lost and that is independent of all the circumstances of time—a kind of timeless present that is contemporaneous with every other present.[25]

Gadamer here uses the classical to explain how one is always being exposed to a text and interpreted by it; in other words, the classical, just as the biblical text is for Luther, is something inescapable, in the sense that we cannot get around its normative power or, in ontological terms, its "gratuity." The principle of *sola scriptura*, contrary to Luther's primary intentions, was not a theory *of* or *for* the biblical text as much as it is a description of the hermeneutical situation in which Dasein is not the interpreter but the interpreted of a remnant. If, as Luther said, "Scripture is not understood, unless it is brought home, that is, experienced,"[26] then interpretation cannot be reduced to elucidation, exegesis, or eisegesis, because it is not concerned mainly with deciphering meanings but with the event of interpretation itself—because the Scripture requires it. Luther indirectly demonstrates how one's relation with a text is primarily hermeneutical-ontological rather than exegetical because Dasein, instead of acting on the text, is listening, responding, and being transformed, because the Scriptures are something over which we do not have control. Gadamer's classical and Luther's Scripture confirm that we have always lived in a world where not what is but what remains is significant, in other words, in a world that is not primarily a realm of objects but of remains to which we are always subordinated.

If Gadamer's classical and Luther's Scripture cannot vanish or disappear but instead remain, independent of all the circumstances of time, it is because "of the effect they have on us," explains Rorty, "not because of the source they came from."[27] The effects, or remains, are more important than the source, because they are what constitute and will continue to constitute the source and its tradition. Tradition is not a fixed structure but rather the historically open-ended intersections of remains. But how is it possible to experience something that *is* not but only remains, such as the classics, Scripture, or even their traditions? The experience of remains is not merely a subjective encounter with an object that rests quietly in itself but is rather an encounter with something that befalls, strikes, and transforms us, as Heidegger explains:

> To undergo an experience with something—be it a thing, a person, or a god—means that this something befalls us, strikes us, comes over us, overwhelms and transforms us. When we talk of

"undergoing" an experience, we mean specifically that the experience is not of our own making; to undergo here means that we endure it, suffer it, receive it as it strikes us and submit to it. It is this something itself that comes about, comes to pass, happens.[28]

Undergoing an experience of remains does not mean having an infinite apprehension of it but only making it endure, which is only possible through listening. And listening does not mean entering into the remains but, on the contrary, belonging to it. In German, the word for listening is also the word for belonging: "we have heard, '*gehört*,' says Heidegger, when we belong to, '*gehören*' what is said."[29] Since we are in a situation where principally there is Being, experience can only be a mode of belonging, that is, an attitude of contemplative listening to Being. In this attitude of contemplative listening Derrida has rightly emphasized "that philosophy finds itself inscribed, rather than inscribing itself, within a space which it seeks but is unable to control, a space which opens out to another which is no longer even *its* other."[30] The space in which philosophy finds itself inscribed is nothing other than its own discursive continuity, which is unable to exert control because it is continually disappearing and appearing, that is, reproducing and producing Being. This difference is nothing other than the remains of Being or, as I said above, the moving verb within it. But why do Being's remnants, through the discursive continuities, indicate also the "space which opens out to another which is no longer even *its* other," hence, to the future generation?

According to Heidegger, "each man is in each instance in dialogue with his forebears, and perhaps even more and in a more hidden manner with those who will come after him,"[31] because hermeneutics in its generative (or constructive) phase always becomes unsatisfiable with respect to whatever it aims at. While something is always left undone in every construction, and because hermeneutics essentially aims to understand what remains undone, it becomes the appropriate philosophy of remnants. Being's remnants are not generated by simple interpretation but as an interpretation that one lives and that carries one forward into the future. But why is it only possible to generate Being from within? In order to explain this, it is necessary to recognize that what remains always presents itself not only as what is always already coming and does not stop coming but also as something that is never anything outside its own folding: a remnant. This is also why Heidegger considered that "we attain an answer to our question only when we remain in conversation with that to which the tradition of philosophy delivers us."[32] Although it is the concrete situation in which we find ourselves to determine the way we are "framed" within metaphysics, it is only from such a frame that Being "remains constantly available to us."[33] Heidegger called on us to settle down and live within metaphysical traditions, languages, and questions because he knew that philosophy could only work out anew Being from within, because the past includes its possibilities: "only what has already been thought prepares what has not yet been thought."[34]

Although "hermeneutics" (from the Greek verb *hermeneuein*), "generation" (from Greek *genesei*), and "within" (from Old English *within-nan*) do not share the same grammatical root, attentive readers will have noticed how I have been using the three terms as synonyms. They all descend from a common ancestor or from an inner part and limit, and all three terms refer to the future, to an unpredictable, unidentifiable, and unpresentable event that I refer to as the remains. The only way to approach such an event is to find the ground of interpretation. But, as Heidegger explained in *Being and Time*, interpretation is grounded in what we have, see, or know, always already and in advance, because it is simply a clarification that produces understanding where it is missing. Understanding only proceeds from the inside, and interpretation is never an explication of objects but only of situations in which we are involved. He specifies:

> Interpretation is never a presuppositionless grasping of something previously given. When the particular concretion of the interpretation in the sense of exact text interpretation likes to appeal to what "is there," what is initially "there" is nothing else than the self-evident, undisputed prejudice of the interpreter, which is necessarily there in each point of departure of the interpretation as what is already "posited" with interpretation as such, that is, pre-given with fore-having, fore-sight, and fore-conception.[35]

Gadamer also insisted that we understand differently if we understand at all because our understanding is determined by the inescapability of history, that is, by the concrete prejudice and situations in which we find ourselves. We cannot stand outside history. History is always intervening from within our own understanding, and when one understands Being differently, it is only because Being's remnants are given to us in another particular situation we are involved in. Hegel also thought that interpretation only occurs within the conceptual order of the one who interprets because, "no one," he said, "can escape the substance of his time any more than he can jump out of his skin."[36] This is the meaning of Hegel's *Aufhebung*: there is no going back in history because it is something that one may only take forward. The point is that if we only exist historically it is because we are in a state, condition, or attitude of *in-between*, that is, a state in which something is called for in the way of "decisions" and "actions" to make and take. Such decisions and actions are similar to the original meaning of *logos* discussed earlier, because both refer to the intrinsic generational procedure of Dasein. As I explain in the introduction, Heidegger called this state, condition, or attitude of Dasein's *in-between* "not a commodity," since it requires that Dasein "in its very being, is in demand, is needed, that he, as the being he is, belongs within a needfulness which claims him . . . with respect to bringing tidings, with respect to preserving a message."[37] This message is Being, and its tidings are the remains of Being, which vary from message to message. The more Dasein focuses on preserving the message, the more messages Being will generate, because it brings tidings, thus news, information, and reports that will always have the postmetaphysical nature of the remains.

As Jean Grondin points out, "there are very few things held in common in the fragmented field of contemporary philosophy, except perhaps for this very fact that we do live in a 'fragmented field' of philosophical discourse, that is, one that is inescapably characterized by interpretation."[38] The fact that the sources or origins of hermeneutics cannot be reduced to a full, disciplined body of thoughts—since they belong to a variety of topics that spread out over many different historical, cultural, and intellectual contexts—makes hermeneutics not only "an-archic" in Schürmann's sense but also "historistic" in Vattimo's sense, because it does not try to take control of Being but seeks rather to appropriate its remains. It is in just this an-archic–historic, fragmented field that our generational hermeneutics is capable of overcoming (*verwinden*, that is, recovering, twisting, incorporating, or learning to live with) other classical philosophical problems linked to the question of Being—such as truth, nominalism, or even relativism—because the ontology of remnants, that is, the weakening of Being, can be used to come to terms with them. As far as relativism is concerned, the doctrine according to which all descriptions of a subject are equally valid, from the point of view of this logic of discursive continuities, preferring one description to another is justified as a response to the description's own historical constellations; in other words, all preferences, decisions, or solutions become responses to the epochal order of the horizons from which they come, thus, "from within." This also is why Heidegger, in *What Is Called Thinking?*, explained that "every way of thinking *takes its way* already *within* the total relation to Being and man's nature, or else it is not thinking at all."[39] If Being is the beginning of a gratuity given to us and it is our task, as thinkers, to make it remain, then it is no surprise that for Heidegger and for most of the six philosophers I studied in the second chapter the human being is the "shepherd of Being,"[40] because they all know, as Hölderlin said in the beginning of the fourth stanza of his hymn "The Rhine," that "as you began, so you will remain [*Wie du anfiengst, wirst du bleiben*]."

NOTES

INTRODUCTION

1. I will translate the German "*Sein*" as "Being," "*Seiend*" as "being," and "*Seiendes*" as "beings." If I use the word "being" with a lowercase *b*, it is because I refer to a definite or indefinite article: e.g., "a being" = "*ein Seiendes*."

2. A very clear exposition of deconstructionism in the philosophical and literary American context can be found in R. Gasché, *Views and Interviews: On "Deconstruction" in America* (Aurora, Colo.: Davies Group, 2007).

3. J. Derrida, *Positions*, trans. A. Bass (London: Continuum, 2002), 9.

4. The list of studies on this theme is enormous. These are some recent titles: G. Stenstad, *Transformations: Thinking After Heidegger* (Madison: University of Wisconsin Press, 2006); D. M. Kleinberg-Levin, *Gestures of Ethical Life: Reading Hölderlin's Question of Measure After Heidegger* (Stanford, Calif.: Stanford University Press, 2005); D. Wood, *Thinking After Heidegger*

(Cambridge: Polity Press, 2002); D. C. Jacobs, *The Presocratics After Heidegger* (Albany: State University of New York Press, 1999); and J. Sallis, *Delimitations: Phenomenology and the End of Metaphysics* (Bloomington: Indiana University Press, 1995).

5. M. Heidegger, *The Essence of Human Freedom: An Introduction to Philosophy*, trans. T. Sadler (London: Continuum, 2002), 198.

6. M. Heidegger, *What Is Philosophy?* trans. J. T. Wilde and W. Kluback (New York: Rowman and Littlefield, 2003), 71–73.

7. This sense of Being is conditioned by the grammatical category that dominates our apprehension of being in the third-person-singular, present-indicative "is." "Is" conceptualizes the infinitive "to be"; that is, it is the third-person-singular ontology that has governed philosophical consciousness and its Being since antiquity.

8. M. Heidegger, *Introduction to Metaphysics*, trans. G. Fried and R. Polt (New Haven, Conn.: Yale University Press, 2000), 35. The translators add a note in their translations explaining that the expression "*Wie steht es um das Sein?*" "could be translated more colloquially as 'What is the status of Being?' or even 'What about Being?' We have kept the German in order to preserve Heidegger's various plays on standing" (35). Note that Heidegger, on pages 25, 27, 28, 29, 30, 32, and 70 of the original German edition uses "*Wie steht es um das Sein?*" and on pages 26, 56, 153, and 154 uses a different formula: "*Wie steht es mit dem Sein?*" Both versions have been translated as "How does it stand with Being?" by the translators. Although I agree with them that there is not a big difference in meaning between the two formulations, I have decided to translate both versions as "How is it going with Being?" because it better captures the postmetaphysical formulation of the question, thus the fact that it has gone through destruction. C. Guignon notes that the "question has a colloquial, almost slangy ring to it" (C. Guignon, "Being as Appearing: Retrieving the Greek Experience of *Phusis*," in

A Companion to Heidegger's Introduction to Metaphysics, ed. R. Polt and G. Fried [New Haven, Conn.: Yale University Press, 2000], 34).

9. M. Heidegger, *The Question Concerning Technology*, trans. W. Lovitt (New York: Harper and Row, 1977), 39.

10. Although Heidegger believes that, before metaphysics began with Plato, there were premetaphysical understandings of Being (pre-Socratic thinkers asked questions concerning the Being of beings but in such a way that Being itself was laid open), I prefer to think of ontology as starting with Plato, because the philological justifications of the pre-Socratic (nonmetaphysical) understandings of Being are too ambiguous.

11. G. Vattimo, *Beyond Interpretation*, trans. D. Webb (Stanford, Calif.: Stanford University Press, 1997), 25.

12. J. Stambaugh, "Heidegger," in *Phenomenology: Dialogues and Bridges*, ed. R. Bruzina and B. Wilshire (Albany: State University of New York Press, 1982), 7.

13. M. Heidegger, *Nietzsche*, trans. D. F. Krell (San Francisco: Harper & Row, 1991), 3:202.

14. G. Vattimo, *Nihilism and Emancipation*, ed. S. Zabala., trans. W. McCuaig (New York: Columbia University Press, 2004), 6.

15. This course was partially published first in *Magazine littéraire* 207 (May 1984): 35–39, and recently as "Qu'est-ce que les Lumières?" in M. Foucault, *Dits et écrits II, 1976–1988* (Paris: Gallimard, 2001), 1498–1507. This edition of the essay was not included in the three-volume English translation of *Dits et écrits* (which includes both editions) edited by P. Rabinow for the New Press. Only the second edition, from 1984, was translated and included in *The Foucault Reader*, edited by P. Rabinow (New York: Pantheon Books, 1984), 32–50; and now in M. Foucault, "What Is Enlightenment?" in *Ethics, Subjectivity, and Truth*, ed. P. Rabinow, trans. R. Hurley and others (New York: New Press, 1997), 304–319. One of the first philosophers

to comment on Foucault's *ontologie de l'actualité* (sometimes translated as "ontology of the present," "ontology of ourselves," or "ontology of current events") was Vincent Descombes, in *The Barometer of Modern Reason: On the Philosophies of Current Events* (1988), trans. Stephen Adam Schwartz (New York: Oxford University Press, 1993), which is an investigation of how philosophy should deal with world events.

16. Foucault, "What Is Enlightenment?"

17. M. Foucault, "On the Genealogy of Ethics: An Overview of Work in Progress," in M. Foucault, *Ethics, Subjectivity, and Truth*, ed. P. Rabinow, trans. R. Hurley and others (New York: New Press, 1997), 253–280.

18. Foucault, "Qu'est-ce que les Lumières?" 1506–1507.

19. Foucault, "What Is Enlightenment?" 315.

20. Ibid.

21. "All my philosophical edification," said Foucault in 1984, "has been determined by the reading Heidegger. . . . Had I not read him, I would not have studied Nietzsche either" (M. Foucault, "Le retour de la morale," in *Dits et écrits II* [Paris: Gallimard, 2001], 1522). This is one of the few interviews not translated in the three-volume English translation of *Dits et écrits*.

22. Vincent Descombes confirms this in his outstanding analysis on Foucault's ontology of actuality: "An ontology of the present must tell us about the present *as* present, about time *as* time, about the unaccomplished *as* unaccomplished, about the past *as* past. Yet conceptual discussions of this order are notoriously absent from Foucault's writings. In keeping with the positivist program, he can only conceive of studying a concept in the historical mode. Which amounts to saying that an *entirely historicist philosophy* may well be political but, prima facie, it has nothing to do with any sort of ontology" (Descombes, *The Barometer of Modern Reason*, 18).

23. I. Hacking, *Historical Ontology* (Cambridge, Mass.: Harvard University Press, 2002).

24. D. D. Roberts, *Nothing but History* (Aurora, Colo.: Davies Group, 2006).

25. Vattimo, *Nihilism and Emancipation*, 87.

26. G. Vattimo, "Toward an Ontology of Decline," trans. B. Spackman, in *Recoding Metaphysics: The New Italian Philosophy*, ed. G. Borradori (Evanston, Ill.: Northwestern University Press, 1988).

27. G. Vattimo, "Ontology of Actuality," in *Contemporary Italian Philosophy*, ed. S. Benso and B. Schroeder (New York: State University of New York Press, 2007), 89–107; G. Vattimo, *Beyond Interpretation: The Meaning of Hermeneutics for Philosophy*, trans. D. Webb (Cambridge: Polity Press, 1997); and Vattimo, *Nihilism and Emancipation*.

28. Vattimo, *Nihilism and Emancipation*, 86. Note that G. L. Bruns and V. Descombes gave formulations very similar to Vattimo's question despite the fact that the question is intended, in Bruns's case, for hermeneutics and, in Descombes's case, for a criticism of modern philosophy, while Vattimo formulated it for ontology. Bruns specified the question by saying, "the main question in hermeneutics is reflective and historical rather than formal and exegetical; the question is not how do we analyze and interpret but how do we respond to hermeneutical situations (or to any situation in which we find ourselves?). A critical form of this question is: How do we stand with respect to all that comes down to us from the past?" (G. L. Bruns, *Hermeneutics: Ancient and Modern* [New Haven, Conn.: Yale University Press, 1992], 195). And Descombes stated that the "heart" of *The Barometer of Modern Reason* is "how can philosophy deal with the world events [*l'actualité*]?" (Descombes, *The Barometer of Modern Reason*, 8).

29. J. Kristeva, "Psychoanalysis and the Polis," in *Transforming the Hermeneutic Context: From Nietzsche to Nancy*, ed. G. L. Ormiston and A. D. Schrift (Albany, N.Y.: SUNY Press, 1990), 99. The recent publication of M. Foucault, *The Hermeneutics of the Subject: Lectures at the College de France, 1981–1982* (London: Palgrave Macmillan, 2005), will be very useful for understand-

ing the significance of hermeneutics in France, which until now has only been attributed to Paul Ricoeur (1913–2005). A very interesting dialogue between Ricoeur and Gadamer can be found in "The Conflict of Interpretations," in *Phenomenology: Dialogues and Bridges*, ed. R. Bruzina and B. Wilshire (Albany, N.Y.: SUNY Press, 1982), 299–320.

30. M. Heidegger, *On the Way to Language*, trans. P. D. Hertz (San Francisco: Harper & Row, 1982), 29.

31. Ibid., 36.

32. Heidegger, *What Is Philosophy?* 67, 69.

33. Ibid., 71.

34. Heidegger, *Introduction to Metaphysics*, 77.

35. Heidegger, in *Introduction to Metaphysics*, referred to Being after deconstruction as the "un-graspable."

36. Heidegger, *Introduction to Metaphysics*, 97.

37. Although Marion is known for his investigations of Descartes, he has devoted a great deal of analysis to ontology and Heidegger, such as *Reduction and Givenness: Investigation of Husserl, Heidegger, and Phenomenology*, trans. T. A. Carlson (Evanston, Ill.: Northwestern University Press, 1998). His most original book, *God Without Being*, trans. T. A. Carlson (Chicago: University of Chicago Press, 1991), is all based on Heidegger's philosophy.

38. On the very first page of his magnum opus, *Being and Event*, trans. Oliver Feltham (New York: Continuum, 2005), Badiou declares that "Heidegger is the last universally recognizable philosopher."

39. E. Lévinas, *Is It Righteous to Be? Interviews with Emmanuel Lévinas*, ed. J. Robbins (Stanford, Calif.: Stanford University Press, 2001), 176. In *Ethics and Infinity*, trans. R. A. Cohen (Pittsburgh, Penn.: Duquesne University Press, 1985), Lévinas goes on to say that a "man who undertakes to philosophize in the twentieth century cannot not have gone through Heidegger's philosophy, even to escape it. This thought is a great event of our century.

Philosophizing without having known Heidegger would involve a share of 'naiveté' in the Husserlian sense of the term" (42).

40. E. Lévinas, *Otherwise Than Being; Or, Beyond Essence*, trans. A. Lingis (Pittsburgh, Penn.: Duquesne University Press, 2004).

41. E. Lévinas, *Totality and Infinity: An Essay on Exteriority*, trans. A. Lingis (Pittsburgh, Penn.: Duquesne University Press, 1969).

42. Ibid., 43.

43. Lévinas, *Is It Righteous to Be?* 105.

44. Lévinas, *Otherwise Than Being*, 42–43.

45. Lévinas, *Is It Righteous to Be?* 250.

46. From J-L. Marion, *God Without Being*, trans. T. A. Carlson (Chicago: University of Chicago Press, 1991), 61. The original is published in M. Heidegger, *Seminare, Gesamtausgabe* (Frankfurt: Vittorio Klostermann, 1986), 15:436–437.

47. M. Heidegger, "Phenomenology and Theology" (1927), in *Pathmarks*, ed. W. McNeill (Cambridge; Cambridge University Press, 1998), 39–62.

48. Marion, *God Without Being*, xx.

49. D. Janicaud, "France: Rendre à nouveau raison?" in *La Philosophie en Europe*, ed. R. Klibansky and D. Pears (Paris: Gallimard/Folio, 1993), 187.

50. Badiou, *Being and Event*, 10.

51. A. Badiou, *Theoretical Writings*, ed. R. Brassier and A. Toscano (New York: Continuum, 2004), xv.

52. Badiou, *Being and Event*. 5.

53. Badiou recorded this objection in *Deleuze: The Clamor of Being*, trans. L. Burchill (Minneapolis: University of Minnesota Press, 1999).

54. Badiou, *Being and Event*. 10.

55. R. Schürmann, *Heidegger on Being and Acting: From Principles to Anarchy*, trans. C-M. Gros (Bloomington: University of Indiana Press, 1990), 284.

56. M. Heidegger, "The End of Philosophy and the Task of Thinking," in *On*

Time and Being, trans. J. Stambaugh (Chicago: University of Chicago Press, 2002), 56.

1. BEING DESTROYED:
HEIDEGGER'S DESTRUCTION OF BEING AS PRESENCE

1. The complete works of Martin Heidegger, *Gesamtausgabe,* are published by Vittorio Klostermann, Frankfurt.

2. Although I will hardly quote any secondary literature on Heidegger, since this chapter does not pretend to be either an introduction to or a faithful interpretation of Heidegger's philosophy, it is important to indicate some essential studies that have been done on some of the concepts I will be discussing here: on the concept of Being, H. Philipse, *Heidegger's Philosophy of Being: A Critical Interpretation* (Princeton, N.J.: Princeton University Press, 1998). On *Being and Time,* T. Kisiel, *The Genesis of Heidegger's* Being and Time (Berkeley: University of California Press, 1993); H. L. Dreyfus, *Being-in-the-World: A Commentary on Heidegger's* Being and Time, *Division I* (Cambridge, Mass.: The MIT Press, 1991); C. Lafont, *Heidegger, Language, and World-Disclosure* (Cambridge, Mass.: The MIT Press, 2000); T. Carman, *Heidegger's Analytic: Interpretation, Discourse, and Authenticity in* Being and Time (Cambridge: Cambridge University Press, 2003). On the concept of truth, O. Dahlstrom, *Heidegger's Concept of Truth* (Cambridge: Cambridge University Press, 2001). On Heidegger's thought in general, W. J. Richardson, *Heidegger: Through Phenomenology to Thought* (New York: Fordham University Press, 2003); G. Steiner, *Martin Heidegger* (Chicago: University of Chicago Press, 1991); J. Van Buren, *The Young Heidegger: Rumor of the Hidden King* (Bloomington: Indiana University Press, 1994); J. E. Faulconer and M. A. Wrathall, eds., *Appropriating Heidegger* (Cambridge: Cambridge University Press, 2000). Indispensable for anyone working on Heidegger today is M. Inwood, *A Heidegger Diction-*

ary (London: Blackwell Publishing, 1999); and Heidegger's biography by R. Safranski, *Martin Heidegger: Between Good and Evil*, trans. E. Osers (Cambridge, Mass.: Harvard University Press, 1998).

3. This is the only passage where Wittgenstein talks about Heidegger: "Apropos of Heidegger: To be sure, I can imagine what Heidegger means by being and anxiety. Man feels the urge to run up against the limits of language. Think for example of the astonishment that anything at all exists. This astonishment cannot be expressed in the form of a question, and there is no answer whatsoever. Nevertheless we do run up against the limits of language. Kierkegaard too saw that there is this running up against something and he referred to it in a fairly similar way (as running against paradox). This running up against the limits of language is ethics. I think it is definitely important to put an end to all the claptrap about ethics— whether intuitive knowledge exists, whether values exist, whether good is definable. In ethics, we are always making the attempt to say something that cannot be said, something that does not and never will touch the essence of the matter. It is a priori certainly that whatever definition of the good may be given it will always be merely a misunderstanding to say that the essential thing, that what is really meant, corresponds to what is expressed. But the inclination, the running up against something, indicates something. What, you swine, you want not to talk nonsense! Go ahead and talk nonsense, is does not matter!" (*Ludwig Wittgenstein and the Circle of Vienna*, ed. B. McGuinness [Oxford: Blackwell, 1979], 68–69).

4. Hermeneutics was certainly not understood by Heidegger as a "philosophy," but we call it this because it has become, since Heidegger, a philosophical position. Either way, Heidegger explained what he intended for hermeneutics in a passage from an early (1923) lecture course: "Hermeneutics is itself not philosophy. It wishes only to place an object which has hitherto fallen into forgetfulness before today's philosophers for their

'well-disposed consideration.' That such minor matters are lost sight of today should not be surprising, given the great industry of philosophy where everything is geared merely to ensuring that one will not come too late for the 'resurrection of metaphysics' which—so one has heard—is now beginning, where one knows only the single care of helping oneself and others to a friendship with the loving God which is as cheap as possible, as convenient as possible, and as profitably direct as possible into the bargain inasmuch as it is transacted through an intuition of essences" (M. Heidegger, *Ontology—the Hermeneutics of Facticity*, trans. J. van Buren [Bloomington: Indiana University Press, 1999], 16).

5. "Amend" should not be understood as "problem-solving" but as "problem-regulating."

6. M. Heidegger, "The End of Philosophy and the Task of Thinking," in *On Time and Being*, trans. J. Stambaugh (Chicago: University of Chicago Press, 2002), 55.

7. M. Heidegger, *Being and Time*, trans. Joan Stambaugh (New York: State University of New York Press, 1996), 23.

8. Luther uses "*destruere*" in his *Heidelberger Disputation*.

9. We now know that in several courses from before and during 1927 Heidegger used the concept of destruction—especially in the 1923 course, *Ontology—the Hermeneutics of Facticity*.

10. M. Heidegger, "Time and Being," in *On Time and Being*, trans. J. Stambaugh (Chicago: University of Chicago Press, 2002), 2.

11. M. Heidegger, *Contributions to Philosophy (From Enowning)* (1989), trans. P. Emad and K. Maly (Bloomington: Indiana University Press, 1999), 154.

12. M. Heidegger, *Introduction to Metaphysics* (1953), trans. G. Fried and R. Polt (New Haven, Conn.: Yale University Press, 2000), 218.

13. M. Heidegger, *The Basic Problems of Phenomenology*, trans. A. Hofstadter (Bloomington: Indiana University Press, 1982), 23.

14. On the difference between *Destruktion* and *déconstruction,* see H.-G. Gadamer's essays "Destruktion and Deconstruction" and "Hermeneutics and
Logocentrism" in *Dialogue and Deconstruction: The Gadamer-Derrida Encounter,* ed. D. P. Michelfelder and R. E. Palmer (Albany: State University
of New York Press, 1989), 102–125; and R. Gasché, *The Tain of the Mirror:
Derrida and the Philosophy of Reflection* (Cambridge, Mass.: Harvard University Press, 1986), who thoughtfully analyzes the origin of destruction
in Husserl, Heidegger, and Derrida. Also R. Bernasconi, "Seeing Double:
Destruktion and Deconstruction," in *Dialogue and Deconstruction,* 233–250,
is very clear on this difference. Among other studies on Heidegger and
Derrida, see G. Stellardi, *Heidegger and Derrida on Philosophy and Metaphor: Imperfect Thought* (New York: Prometheus Books, 2000); H. Rapaport, *Heidegger and Derrida: Reflections on Time and Language* (Lincoln:
University of Nebraska Press, 1991); and the recent investigation by P. Marrati, *Genesis and Trace: Derrida Reading Husserl and Heidegger* (Stanford,
Calif.: Stanford University Press, 2005).

15. J. Derrida, *Points . . . Interviews, 1974–1994,* ed. E. Weber, trans. P. Kamuf
and others (Stanford, Calif.: Stanford University Press, 1995), 211.

16. J. Derrida, *Paper Machine,* trans. R. Bowlby (Stanford, Calif.: Stanford University Press, 2005), 117.

17. Derrida, *Points,* 83.

18. Ibid., 211.

19. Derrida, *Paper Machine,* 115.

20. J. Derrida, "A Discussion with Jacques Derrida," *Writing Instructor* 9, nos.
1–2 (Fall 1989–Winter 1990): 18. Derrida went on to explain that one "must
remember the Nietzschean, Freudian, and above all Heideggerian premis-
es of deconstruction. And especially, in relation to Heidegger, that there is
a Christian, or more precisely a Lutheran tradition of what Heidegger calls
Destruktion. Luther, as I describe in my book on Jean-Luc Nancy and what

Nancy calls the 'deconstruction of Christianity,' was already talking about *destruction* to designate the need for a desedimentation of the theological strata hiding the original nakedness of the evangelical message to be restored. What interests me more and more is to make out the specificity of a deconstruction that wouldn't necessarily be reducible to this Lutheran-Heideggerian tradition" (Derrida, *Paper Machine*, 137–138).

21. Heidegger, *Being and Time*, 20.

22. Ibid., 23.

23. Ibid., 22–23.

24. M. Heidegger, *Zollikon Seminars, 1959–1969*, ed. M. Boss, trans. F. Mayr and R. Askay (Evanston, Ill.: Northwestern University Press, 2001), 117.

25. Ibid., 118.

26. Heidegger, *Being and Time*, 10. "Dasein" is Heidegger's way of characterizing the being of humans and the entity or person who has this being.

27. Heidegger, *On the Way to Language*, trans. P. D. Hertz (New York: Harper and Row, 1982), 32.

28. Ibid., 40.

29. Heidegger, *Being and Time*, 20.

30. M. Heidegger, *The Principle of Reason* (1957), trans. R. Lilly (Bloomington: University of Indiana Press, 1996).

31. Heidegger, *Contributions to Philosophy (From Enowning)*, 76.

32. M. Heidegger, "Only a God Can Save Us," in *Philosophical and Political Writings*, ed. M. Stassen (New York: Continuum, 2003), 38.

33. In a famous essay entitled "Overcoming Metaphysics," Heidegger explained the relation between the oblivion of Being regarding the realization of war: "The 'world wars' and their character of 'totality' are already a consequence of the abandonment of Being. They press toward guarantee of the stability of a constant form of using things up. Man, who no longer conceals his character of being the most important raw material, is

also drawn into this process. Man is the 'most important raw material' because he remains the subject of all consumption. He does this in such a way that he lets his will be unconditionally equated with this process, and thus at the same time become the 'object' of the abandonment of Being. The world wars are the antecedent form of the removal of the difference between war and peace. This removal is necessary since the 'world' has become an unworld as a consequence of the abandonment of beings by Being's truth" (M. Heidegger, "Overcoming Metaphysics," in *The End of Philosophy*, trans. J. Stambaugh [New York: Harper and Row, 1973], 103–104).

34. M. Heidegger, *What Is Called Thinking?* trans. J. Glenn Gray (New York: Harper and Row, 1968), 80.

35. This term is used by Heidegger to evade classical philosophical connotations attached to the notion of the subject, by giving the most basic sense possible of what it means to "exist" as a conscious being. Rocks do not exist in the same sense we do. Since the seventeenth century, the infinitive was nominalized as (*das*) *Dasein* originally in the sense of some "presence," and since the eighteenth century it started to be used as an alternative to the Latinate *existenz* (the existence of God or of life). Dasein is essentially temporal, and this characteristic is derived from its tripartite ontological structure: *existence, thrownness*, and *fallenness*.

36. "Thrownness" refers to the fact that Dasein always finds itself already in a certain spiritual and material, historically conditioned environment, thus, in the world, in which the space of possibilities is always historically limited. It represents the phenomenon of the past as having-been. Dasein's "fallenness" characterizes its existence in the midst of beings that are both Dasein and not Dasein. "Existence" means that Dasein is potentiality-for-being, *Seinkönnen*; it projects its being upon various possibilities, especially the phenomenon of the future.

37. Heidegger, *Contributions to Philosophy (From Enowning)*, 23.

38. Heidegger, *Being and Time*, 3.

39. Heidegger, *Introduction to Metaphysics*, 86.

40. Heidegger, *On the Way to Language*, 34.

41. Heidegger, *Being and Time*, 3.

42. This is the passage from *Being and Time* where Heidegger explains the significance of the ontological difference: "The distinction between the being of existing Dasein and the being of beings unlike Dasein (for example, reality) may seem to be illuminating, but it is only the *point of departure* for the ontological problematic; it is nothing with which philosophy can rest and be satisfied" (397). It is interesting to note a testimony by Gadamer that shows how the ontological difference is not something that can really be neglected, because it is always happening: "I still recall," says Gadamer, "quite clearly how, in Marburg, the young Heidegger developed this concept of the 'ontological difference' in the sense of the difference between being and beings, between *ousia* and *on*. One day, as Gerhard Krüger and I accompanied Heidegger home, one of the two of us raised the question of what, then, the significance of this ontological distinction was, how and when one must make this distinction. I will never forget Heidegger's answer: Make? Is the ontological difference something that must be made? That is a misunderstanding. This difference is not something introduced by the philosopher's thinking so as to distinguish between being and beings" (H.-G. Gadamer, *The Beginning of Philosophy*, trans. R. Coltman [New York: Continuum, 2001], 123).

43. Heidegger, *Being and Time*, 16.

44. Ibid., 10.

45. Ibid., 18.

46. M. Heidegger, *Kant and the Problem of Metaphysics* (1929), trans. R. Taft (Bloomington: Indiana University Press, 1997), 143.

47. Heidegger, *Being and Time*, 352.

48. M. Heidegger, *The Essence of Human Freedom* (1930), trans. T. Sadler (London: Continuum, 2002), 198.

49. M. Heidegger, *The Fundamental Concepts of Metaphysics: World, Finitude, Solitude,* trans. W. McNeill and N. Walker (Bloomington: Indiana University Press, 1994), 352.

50. Heidegger, *Being and Time,* 39.

51. Heidegger, *Contributions to Philosophy (From Enowning),* 98.

52. Heidegger, "Only a God Can Save Us," 37.

53. This is the passage in *Being and Time*: "Philosophy is universal phenomenological ontology, taking its departure from the hermeneutic of Dasein, which, as an analysis of *existence*, has fastened the end of the guideline of all philosophical inquiry at the point from which it *arises* and to which it *returns*" (34).

54. M. Heidegger, "Letter on 'Humanism,'" in *Pathmarks* (1967), ed. W. McNeill (Cambridge, Mass.: The MIT Press, 2002), 261.

55. In the essay "Time and Being," Heidegger justifies this by saying that "the only possible way to anticipate the latter thought on the destiny of Being from the perspective of *Being and Time* is to think through what was presented in *Being and Time* about the dismantling [which is another word for destroying] of the ontological doctrine of the Being of beings" (Heidegger, "Time and Being," in *On Time and Being,* 6).

56. Heidegger, "Only a God Can Save Us," 38.

57. M. Heidegger, *Basic Concepts,* trans. G. E. Aylesworth (Bloomington: Indiana University Press, 1993), 51–52.

58. Heidegger, "Only a God Can Save Us," 37.

59. Heidegger, "Letter on 'Humanism,'" 241.

60. Heidegger, "Only a God Can Save Us," 42.

61. Heidegger, "Letter on 'Humanism,'" 239.

62. Ibid., 251.

63. Heidegger, "Overcoming Metaphysics," in *The End of Philosophy*, 97.

64. Heidegger, *Contributions to Philosophy (From Enowning)*, 60.

65. Heidegger, *What Is Called Thinking?* 137.

66. Heidegger, "Overcoming Metaphysics," 90.

67. Heidegger, "Letter on 'Humanism,'" 250.

68. Heidegger, "Overcoming Metaphysics," 91.

69. Heidegger, "Time and Being," in *On Time and Being*, 24.

70. Heidegger, *The End of Philosophy*, includes "Metaphysics as History of Being," "Sketches for a History of Being as Metaphysics," "Recollection in Metaphysics" (all three included now in volume 2 of Heidegger's *Nietzsche*), and "Overcoming Metaphysics" (from Heidegger's *Vorträge und Aufsätze*).

71. Heidegger, introduction to *The End of Philosophy*, xiii.

72. M. Heidegger, *Identity and Difference*, trans. J. Stambaugh (Chicago: University of Chicago Press, 1969), 48.

73. Ibid., 50.

74. Ibid., 52.

75. Heidegger, *Basic Concepts*, 51.

76. Heidegger, "Overcoming Metaphysics," in *The End of Philosophy*, 85.

77. Heidegger, "Letter on 'Humanism,'" 239.

78. Heidegger, *Being and Time*, 211.

79. Heidegger, "Time and Being," 6.

80. Ibid., 9.

81. Ibid., 19.

82. Ibid., 21.

83. Heidegger, *Basic Concepts*, 52.

84. Ibid.

85. Heidegger, *Being and Time*, xvii.

86. Heidegger, *Introduction to Metaphysics*, 35. As I write in the introduction, note 8, I have made a small change to the translation of this question.

87. Heidegger, *Introduction to Metaphysics*, 38. Heidegger is quoting Nietzsche, *Twilight of the Idols*, §4, " 'Reasons' in Philosophy."

88. Heidegger, *Introduction to Metaphysics*, 41.

89. Heidegger, *Basic Concepts*, 52.

90. Heidegger, *Introduction to Metaphysics*, 77.

91. Note that in all the Heideggerian secondary literature I have studied, only Steiner (in *Martin Heidegger*, 40) and Derrida (in *Of Spirit: Heidegger and the Question* [1987] and "The Supplement of Copula: Philosophy Before Linguistics" [1971], included in his *Margins of Philosophy*) have emphasized the significance of this prior question. Marrati has recently also analyzed this question in relation to the problem of the origin in Heidegger (in *Genesis and Trace*, 109–139).

92. Heidegger, *Introduction to Metaphysics*, 216.

93. Heidegger, *Basic Concepts*, 52.

94. Heidegger, *Introduction to Metaphysics*, 219.

95. Ibid., 44.

96. Heidegger, "Letter on 'Humanism,' " 239.

97. Heidegger, *On the Way to Language*, 30.

98. Contrary to Descartes' and Husserl's cognitive and theoretical traditional attitude toward the world, it is "care" that is Dasein's essential attitude and that determines its relation to the world. "Factical Dasein exists as born, and, born, it is already dying in the sense of being-toward-death. Both 'ends' and their 'between' are as long as Dasein factically exists, and they are in the sole way possible on the basis of the Being of Dasein as care" (Heidegger, *Being and Time*, 343).

99. Heidegger, *Introduction to Metaphysics*, 144.

100. Ibid., 97.

101. Ibid., 90.

102. Ibid., 86.

2. AFTER THE DESTRUCTION: THE REMAINS OF BEING

1. See O. Pöggeler, *The Paths of Heidegger's Life and Thought*, trans. J. Baliff (Atlantic Highlands, N.J.: Humanities Press, 1998); R. P. Pippin, *Modernism as a Philosophical Problem* (Oxford: Blackwell, 1991); and G. Vattimo, *Beyond Interpretation*, trans. D. Webb (Stanford, Calif.: Stanford University Press, 1997).

2. Although Heidegger criticized such truth theory in several courses, it is in *Being and Time* that his criticism is first brought forward in relation to the statement "truth by no means has the structure of an agreement between knowing and the object in the sense of a correspondence of one Being (subject) to another (object)" (Heidegger, *Being and Time*, 201).

3. Heidegger, *Introduction to Metaphysics*, 90.

4. M. Heidegger, "The Origin of the Work of Art," in *Off the Beaten Track*, ed. and trans. J. Young and K. Haynes (Cambridge: Cambridge University Press 2002), 37.

5. This "turn" is supposed to indicate a certain shift within Heidegger's philosophy, from understanding being from the standpoint of Dasein to an understanding of being from the standpoint of being itself. I do not believe such a change actually occurred, and I am convinced that it is clear that even the early Heidegger understood Dasein only from the standpoint of being itself.

6. M. Heidegger, "Anaximander's Saying," in *Off the Beaten Track*, ed. and trans. J. Young and K. Haynes (Cambridge: Cambridge University Press 2002), 275.

7. Ibid.

8. Heidegger, "Time and Being," in *On Time and Being*, 3.

9. Heidegger, "Anaximander's Saying," 275.

10. Derrida, *Paper Machine*, 151–152.

11. Ibid., 152.

12. Heidegger, "Overcoming Metaphysics," in *The End of Philosophy*, 91.

13. Just as the first chapter did not pretend to be a faithful interpretation of Heidegger's philosophy, neither does this second chapter pretend to introduce these authors' thought. A clear and complete introduction to these philosophers may be found in the following texts: On Schürmann, the essays by R. Bernasconi, D. Janicaud, J. Sallis, R. Gasché, M. Harr, and others, in "Memory of Reiner Schürmann," *Graduate Faculty Philosophy Journal* 19–20, no. 2 (1981) and no. 1 (1997); and A. Martinengo, *Introduzione a Reiner Schürmann* (Rome: Meltemi, 2008). On Derrida: B. Stocker, *Routledge Philosophy Guidebook to Derrida on Deconstruction* (London: Routledge, 2006); and N. Lucy, *A Derrida Dictionary* (Oxford: Blackwell, 2004). On Nancy: I. James, *The Fragmentary Demand: An Introduction to the Philosophy of Jean-Luc Nancy* (Stanford, Calif.: Stanford University Press, 2006). On Gadamer: J. Grondin, *The Philosophy of Gadamer* (Montreal: McGill-Queen's University Press, 2003). On Tugendhat: S. Zabala, *The Hermeneutic Nature of Analytic Philosophy: A Study of Ernst Tugendhat* (New York: Columbia University Press, 2008). On Vattimo: M. Frascati-Lochhead, *Kenosis and Feminist Theology: The Challenge of Gianni Vattimo* (Albany, N.Y.: SUNY Press, 1998); G. Giorgio, *Il pensiero di Gianni Vattimo. L'emancipazione dalla metafisica tra dialettica ed ermeneutica* (Milan: Franco Angeli, 2006); and the essays by U. Eco, R. Rorty, C. Taylor, J. Miles, C. Dotolo, and others in *Weakening Philosophy: Essays in Honour of Gianni Vattimo*, ed. S. Zabala (Montreal: McGill-Queen's University Press, 2006).

14. R. Schürmann, "Deconstruction Is Not Enough: On Gianni Vattimo's Call for 'Weak Thinking,'" *Graduate Faculty Philosophy Journal* 10 (1984): 173.

15. R. Schürmann, *On Being and Acting: From Principles to Anarchy*, trans. C.-M. Gros (Bloomington: University of Indiana Press, 1990), 10.

16. R. Schürmann, "Questioning the Foundations of Practical Philosophy," in

Phenomenology Dialogues and Bridges, ed. R. Bruzina and B. Wilshire (Albany, N.Y.: State University of New York Press, 1982), 12.

17. Schürmann, "Questioning the Foundations of Practical Philosophy," 12.

18. R. Schürmann, "Deconstruction Is Not Enough," 172.

19. Ibid., 173.

20. Schürmann, *Heidegger on Being and Acting*, 41.

21. Ibid., 301. Schürmann's main point is not only to show that thinking means remembering, recalling the birth of an epoch and the sequence of ancestors that established its filiations, but to point out that when a historical world falls in place, another epoch takes over with a new dwelling. This new dwelling, or arrangement, produces a new *nomos* of our *oikos*, a new "economy," which can best be recalled as an economic thinking. He illustrates what "economic thinking" is in this significant passage: "The Parthenon: within the network of actions, things, and words, the way an entity like the Acropolis is present epochally assumed a well-defined, although complex character—when rhapsodes prepared for the Panathenean festival, when the Parthenon served as a Byzantine church, when the Turks used it as a powder magazine. Today, when it has become a commodity for tourist consumption and when UNESCO plans to protect it from pollution with a plastic dome, it is present in an epochal economy in yet another fashion—a mode of presence certainly inconceivable for its architect, Ichtynos. At each moment of this history, the edifice was present according to finite, unforeseeable, uncontrollable traits. And each entailed the irremediable disappearance of such an epochal physiognomy" (Schürmann, *Heidegger on Being and Acting*, 57).

22. Ibid., 49.

23. Schürmann, "Questioning the Foundations of Practical Philosophy," 13.

24. Ibid., 18.

25. Schürmann, *Heidegger on Being and Acting*, 145.

26. Ibid., 50.

27. Ibid., 295.

28. Ibid., 273.

29. Ibid., 228.

30. Schürmann, "Questioning the Foundations of Practical Philosophy," 16.

31. Schürmann, *Heidegger on Being and Acting*, 150.

32. Ibid., 25.

33. Schürmann, "Questioning the Foundations of Practical Philosophy," 18.

34. Ibid., 19.

35. Schürmann, *Heidegger on Being and Acting*, 149.

36. *Broken Hegemonies* is the title of Schürmann's 1996 book.

37. Schürmann, *Heidegger on Being and Acting*, 286.

38. Ibid., 284.

39. Ibid., 297.

40. J. Derrida, *Of Grammatology*, trans. G. Chakravorty Spivak (Baltimore, Md.: The John Hopkins University Press, 1997), 12.

41. J. Derrida, *Margins of Philosophy*, trans. A. Bass (Chicago: University of Chicago Press, 1982), 177.

42. Ibid., 125.

43. Derrida, *Points*, 374.

44. Ibid., 145.

45. Ibid., 149.

46. Ibid., 211.

47. Derrida, *Positions*, 9.

48. Derrida, *Margins of Philosophy*, 66–67.

49. Ibid., 66.

50. Ibid., 24.

51. Ibid.

52. M. Heidegger, "Anaximander's Saying" (1946), in *Off the Beaten Track*,

trans. J. Young and K. Haynes (Cambridge: Cambridge University Press, 2002), 278.

53. Derrida, *Margins of Philosophy*, 25–26.

54. Derrida, *Paper Machine*, 159.

55. Derrida, *Of Grammatology*, 22.

56. Derrida, *Margins of Philosophy*, 3.

57. Ibid., 22.

58. Ibid., 5.

59. Derrida, *Of Grammatology*, 62–63.

60. Derrida, *Positions*, 26.

61. Derrida, *Margins of Philosophy*, 11.

62. Derrida, *Points*, 208.

63. Derrida explained that "the words I had somewhat privileged up till now, such as trace, writing, gramme, turned out to be better named by 'cinder' for the following reason: Ashes or cinders are obviously traces—in general, the first figure of the trace one thinks of is that of the step, along a path, the step that leaves a footprint, a trace, or a vestige; but 'cinder' renders better what I meant to say with the name of trace, namely, something that remains without remaining, which is neither present nor absent, which destroys itself, which is totally consumed, which is a remainder without remainder" (Derrida, *Points*, 208).

64. Derrida, *Margins of Philosophy*, 5, 6.

65. J.-L. Nancy, *The Birth to Presence*, trans. B. McDonald (Stanford, Calif.: Stanford University Press, 1993), 84.

66. J.-L. Nancy, *A Finite Thinking*, ed. S. Sparks (Stanford, Calif.: Stanford University Press, 2003), 101.

67. Ibid., 10.

68. Ibid., 87.

69. J.-L. Nancy, "The Deconstruction of Christianity," in *Religion and Media*,

ed. H. de Vries and S. Weber (Stanford, Calif.: Stanford University Press, 2001), 121.

70. Nancy, *A Finite Thinking*, 87.

71. Nancy, "The Deconstruction of Christianity," 122.

72. Nancy, *The Birth to Presence*, 4, 5.

73. Nancy, *A Finite Thinking*, 13.

74. J.-L. Nancy, *The Sense of the World*, trans. J. S. Librett (Minneapolis: University of Minnesota Press, 1997), 35. Note that Nancy entitled an essay for the catalogue of the Italian artist Claudio Parmiggiani "What Remains of an Eternal and Fragile Art" ("Ciò che resta di un'arte eterna e fragile," in *Galleria d'Arte Moderna, Bologna. 23 gennaio–30 marzo 2003*, by Claudio Parmiggiani, ed. Peter Weiermair [Milan: Silvana editoriale, 2003], 151–160).

75. Nancy, *The Sense of the World*, 132.

76. Nancy, *A Finite Thinking*, 185.

77. Nancy, *The Birth to Presence*, 38.

78. This is the title of an essay by Nancy included in *The Birth to Presence*.

79. Nancy, *Being Singular Plural*, trans. R. D. Richardson (Stanford, Calif.: Stanford University Press, 2000), 27.

80. Being is a participle or noun, "singular" and "plural" are nouns or adjectives, and all can be rearranged in different combinations.

81. Nancy, *Being Singular Plural*, 37.

82. Ibid., 32.

83. Ibid., 62–63.

84. Ibid., 83.

85. Ibid., 26.

86. Ibid., 46–47.

87. Ibid., 2.

88. Nancy, *The Sense of the World*, 28.

89. Nancy has analyzed community in *The Inoperative Community*, ed. P. Connor (Minneapolis: University of Minnesota Press, 1991).

90. Nancy, *A Finite Thinking*, 268.

91. Nancy, *The Birth to Presence*, 166.

92. Nancy, *Being Singular Plural*, 85.

93. H-G. Gadamer, *Das Erbe Europas* (Frankfurt: Suhrkamp, 1989), 166–173.

94. H-G. Gadamer, *Gadamer in Conversation: Reflections and Commentary*, ed. Richard Palmer (New Haven, Conn.: Yale University Press, 2003), 56.

95. H-G. Gadamer, *The Philosophy of Hans-Georg Gadamer*, ed. L. E. Hahn (Chicago: Open Court Press, 1997), 22.

96. H-G. Gadamer, *Truth and Method*, trans. J. Weinsheimer and D. G. Marshall (London: Continuum, 2004), 470.

97. H-G. Gadamer, *The Gadamer Reader: A Bouquet of the Later Writings*, ed. J. Grondin, trans. R. E. Palmer (Evanston, Ill.: Northwestern University Press, 2007), 371.

98. Gadamer, *Truth and Method*, 248.

99. Gadamer, *The Gadamer Reader*, 365.

100. Gadamer, *The Philosophy of Hans-Georg Gadamer*, 171.

101. Gadamer, *The Gadamer Reader*, 382.

102. H-G. Gadamer, *Dialogue and Deconstruction: The Gadamer-Derrida Encounter*, ed. D. P. Michelfelder and R. E. Palmer (Albany: State University of New York Press, 1989), 100.

103. Ibid., 117.

104. Having said this, although most translators have translated "*Gespräch*" as "conversation," in the few places where it has been translated as dialogue, I will change it to "conversation" in quotation marks in this book.

105. Gadamer, *The Gadamer Reader*, 371.

106. Gadamer, *Truth and Method*, 443.

107. Ibid., 449.

108. Ibid., 391.

109. Gadamer, *Gadamer in Conversation*, 51.

110. H-G. Gadamer, *A Century of Philosophy: Hans-Georg Gadamer in Conversation with Riccardo Dottori*, trans. R. Coltman with S. Koepke (New York: Continuum, 2004), 77.

111. Gadamer, "Reply to Stanley Rosen," in *The Philosophy of Hans-Georg Gadamer*, 221.

112. H-G. Gadamer, *Philosophical Hermeneutics*, trans. D. E. Linge (Berkeley: University of California Press, 1976), 9.

113. Gadamer, *The Gadamer Reader*, 384.

114. Gadamer, "Reflections on My Philosophical Journey," in *The Philosophy of Hans-Georg Gadamer*, 30.

115. Gadamer, *Gadamer in Conversation*, 68.

116. Gadamer, *Dialogue and Deconstruction*, 95.

117. Ibid., 118.

118. Ibid., 122.

119. H-G. Gadamer, "Die Stellung der Philosophie in der Gesellschaft," in *Hermeneutik im Rückblick* (Tübingen: Mohr Siebeck, 1995), 369.

120. E. Tugendhat, *Traditional and Analytical Philosophy: Lectures on the Philosophy of Language*, trans. P. A. Gorner (Cambridge: Cambridge University Press, 1982).

121. Ibid., 74.

122. Ibid., 63.

123. Ibid., 4.

124. Ibid., 8.

125. Tugendhat, *Self-Consciousness and Self-Determination*, 30.

126. E. Tugendhat, preface to the Italian edition of *Traditional and Analytical Philosophy: Lectures on the Philosophy of Language* (Genova: Marietti, 1989), 4.

127. Tugendhat, *Traditional and Analytical Philosophy*, 31.

128. Ibid.

129. E. Tugendhat, "The Dissolution of Ontology Into Formal Semantics," in *The Hermeneutic Nature of Analytic Philosophy: A Study of Ernst Tugendhat*, by S. Zabala (New York: Columbia University Press, 2008), 98.

130. Tugendhat, *Traditional and Analytical Philosophy*, 33.

131. Tugendhat, "The Dissolution of Ontology Into Formal Semantics," 105.

132. Tugendhat, *Traditional and Analytical Philosophy*, 63.

133. Tugendhat, *Self-Consciousness and Self-Determination*, 144.

134. Tugendhat, *Traditional and Analytical Philosophy*, 107.

135. Tugendhat, *Self-Consciousness and Self-Determination*, 149.

136. Heidegger, "What Is Metaphysics?" in *Pathmarks*, 82–96.

137. Tugendhat, *Self-Consciousness and Self-Determination*, 150.

138. Tugendhat, "Phenomenology and Linguistic Analysis," in *Husserl: Expositions and Appraisals*, ed. F. Elliston and P. McCormick (Notre Dame, Ind.: University of Notre Dame Press, 1977), 332.

139. Tugendhat, *Traditional and Analytical Philosophy*, 29.

140. Ibid., 63.

141. The function of a singular term is to pick out one thing from a plurality as what is meant, that is, "as that to which the predicate is supposed to apply" (Tugendhat, *Traditional and Analytical Philosophy*, 239).

142. E. Tugendhat, "Language Analysis and the Critique of Ontology," trans. J. S. Fulton and K. Kolenda, in *Contemporary German Philosophy*, ed. D. E. Christensen (State College: Pennsylvania State University Press, 1983), 2:110–111.

143. Vattimo, *Nihilism and Emancipation*, 3–4.

144. Although this is Vattimo's response, I should point out Vattimo has also once used the expression "residues" by stating that "what becomes truly

human is the tending to what has been, to the residues, to the traces of the lived" (G. Vattimo, "Bottle, Net, Truth, Revolution," *Denver Quarterly* 16 [1982]: 26). Also, C. Dotolo in his book on Vattimo notes in the Italian master's "nihilistic hermeneutics the possibility to turn to the surviving residues" (C. Dotolo, *La teologia fondamentale davanti alle sfide del "pensiero deboole di G. Vattimo"* [Rome: LAS, 1999], 393).

145. G. Vattimo, *The End of Modernity: Nihilism and Hermeneutics in Postmodern Culture*, trans. J. R. Snyder (Baltimore, Md.: The John Hopkins University Press, 1988), 86.

146. G. Vattimo, "Weak Thought and the Reduction of Violence: A Dialogue with Gianni Vattimo by S. Zabala," *Common Knowledge* 3 (2002): 463.

147. G. Vattimo, *The Adventure of Difference: Philosophy After Nietzsche and Heidegger*, trans. C. P. Blamires and T. Harrison (Cambridge: Polity Press, 1993), 5.

148. G. Vattimo, "Foreword," in Zabala, *The Hermeneutic Nature of Analytical Philosophy*, xvi.

149. G. Vattimo, foreword to F. D'Agostini, *Analitici e continentali. Guida alla filosofia degli ultimi trent'anni* (Milan: Cortina, 1997), xv.

150. G. Vattimo, "Dialectics, Difference, and Weak Thought," *Graduate Faculty Philosophy Journal* 10 (1984): 151.

151. Vattimo, *The Adventure of Difference*, 149.

152. G. Vattimo, "Difference and Interference: On the Reduction of Hermeneutics to Anthropology," *Res* 4 (1982): 87.

153. Ibid., 88.

154. Vattimo, "Dialectics, Difference, and Weak Thought," 156.

155. Vattimo, *The End of Modernity*, 156.

156. Vattimo, *Nihilism and Emancipation*, xxv–xxvi.

157. Vattimo, *The End of Modernity*, 121.

158. Vattimo, *The Adventure of Difference*, 150.

159. Vattimo, *Beyond Interpretation*, 105.

160. Ibid., 110–111.

3. GENERATING BEING THROUGH INTERPRETATION:
THE HERMENEUTIC ONTOLOGY OF REMNANTS

1. Heidegger, *Ontology: The Hermeneutics of Facticity*, 14.

2. M. Heidegger, *Heraclitus Seminar*, trans. C. H. Seibert (Evanston, Ill.: Northwestern University Press, 1993), 17.

3. Heidegger, *On the Way to Language*, xx.

4. Bruns, *Hermeneutics: Ancient and Modern*, 61.

5. In *Hermeneutics: Ancient and Modern*.

6. Plato *Symposium* 207c–208a.

7. G. Vattimo, "Nietzsche and Heidegger," *Stanford Italian Review* 6 (1986): 28–29.

8. Derrida, *Positions*, 27.

9. G. Vattimo, *After Christianity*, trans. L. D'Isanto (New York: Columbia University Press, 2002), 67.

10. Ibid., 67–68.

11. Ibid., 68.

12. Heidegger, *Pathmarks*, 217.

13. Heidegger, *The Basic Problems of Phenomenology*, 73.

14. Schürmann, *Heidegger on Being and Acting*, 176.

15. Ibid.

16. Vattimo, "Dialectics, Difference, and Weak Thought," 152.

17. Vattimo, "Toward an Ontology of Decline," 67.

18. Ibid., 70.

19. Heidegger, *Contributions to Philosophy (From Enowning)*, 336.

20. Derrida, *Paper Machine*, 134.

21. Vattimo, *The Adventure of Difference*, 22.

22. Schürmann, *Heidegger on Being and Acting*, 49.

23. Heidegger, *Being and Time*, 20.

24. Heidegger, *Introduction to Metaphysics*, 44.

25. Gadamer, *Truth and Method*, 288.

26. M. Luther, *Dr. Martin Luthers Tischreden (1531–46)* (Weimar: Hermann Böhlaus, 1914), 3:170.

27. R. Rorty and G. Vattimo, *The Future of Religion*, ed. Santiago Zabala (New York: Columbia University Press, 2005), 61.

28. Heidegger, *On the Way to Language*, 57.

29. M. Heidegger, *Early Greek Thinking*, trans. D. F. Krell and F. A. Capuzzi (New York: Harper & Row, 1975), 66.

30. J. Derrida, "The Time of a Thesis: Punctuations," in *Philosophy in France Today*, ed. A. Montefiore, trans. K. McLaughlin (Cambridge: Cambridge University Press, 1983), 45.

31. Heidegger, *On the Way to Language*, 31.

32. Heidegger, *What Is Philosophy?* 71.

33. Heidegger, *Basic Concepts*, 51.

34. Heidegger, *Identity and Difference*, 48.

35. Heidegger, *Being and Time*, 141.

36. G. W. F. Hegel, *Introduction to the Lectures on the History of Philosophy*, trans. T. M. Knox and A. V. Miller (Oxford: Clarendon Press, 1985), 60.

37. Heidegger, *On the Way to Language*, 31.

38. J. Grondin, *Sources of Hermeneutics* (Albany, N.Y.: SUNY Press, 1995), 1.

39. Heidegger, *What Is Called Thinking?* 80.

40. Heidegger, "Letter on Humanism," 252.

BIBLIOGRAPHY

Allen, Barry. *Knowledge and Civilization.* Introduction by Richard Rorty. Boulder, Colo.: Westview Press, 2004.

———. *Truth in Philosophy.* Cambridge, Mass.: Harvard University Press, 1993.

Badiou, Alain. *Being and Event.* Translated by Oliver Feltham. New York: Continuum, 2005.

———. *Deleuze: The Clamor of Being.* Translated by Louise Burchill. Minnesota: University of Minnesota Press, 1999.

———. *Manifesto for Philosophy.* Edited by Norman Madarasz. New York: State University of New York Press, 1999.

———. *Theoretical Writings.* Edited by Ray Brassier and Alberto Toscano. New York: Continuum, 2004.

Barker, Jason. *Alain Badiou: A Critical Introduction.* London: Pluto Press, 2002.

Bernasconi, Robert. *The Question of Language in Heidegger's History of Being.* New York: Prometheus, 1989.

——. "Seeing Double: Destruktion and Deconstruction." In *Dialogue and Deconstruction: The Gadamer-Derrida Encounter,* ed. D. P. Michelfelder and R. E. Palmer, 233–250. New York: State University of New York Press, 1989.

Birault, Henri. *Heidegger et l'expérience de la pensée.* Paris: Gallimard, 1978.

Borradori, Giovanna. *Recoding Metaphysics: The New Italian Philosophy.* Evanston, Ill.: Northwestern University Press, 1988.

Bowie, Andrew. *Introduction to German Philosophy: From Kant to Habermas.* London: Polity Press, 2003.

Brandom, Robert. *Articulating Reasons: An Introduction to Inferentialism.* Cambridge, Mass.: Harvard University Press, 2000.

——. "Hegelian Pragmatism and Social Emancipation. An Interview with Robert Brandom by Italo Testa." *Constellations* 10, no. 4 (December 2003): 554–570.

——. "Interview with R. Brandom by Carlo Penco." *Epistemologia* 22 (1999): 143–150.

——. *Making It Explicit.* Cambridge, Mass.: Harvard University Press, 1994.

——, ed. *Rorty and His Critics.* Oxford: Blackwell, 2000.

——. *Tales of the Mighty Death: Historical Essays in the Metaphysics of Intentionality.* Cambridge, Mass.: Harvard University Press, 2002.

Brogan W, and D. J. Schmidt, eds. *Heidegger and Aristotle: The Twofoldness of Being.* New York: State University of New York Press, 2005.

Bruns, Gerald L. *Hermeneutics: Ancient and Modern.* New Haven, Conn.: Yale University Press, 1992.

Bruzina, R., and B. Wilshire, eds. *Phenomenology: Dialogues and Bridges.* Albany: State University of New York Press, 1982.

Bubner, Rüdiger. *Essays in Hermeneutics and Critical Theory.* Translated by Eric Matthews. New York: Columbia University Press, 1988.

———. *Modern German Philosophy.* Cambridge: Cambridge University Press, 1981.

———. "Zur Wirkung der analytischen Philosophie in Deutschland." In *Die sog: Geisteswissenschaften*, ed. W. Prinz and P. Weingart, 448–458. Frankfurt: M. Suhrkamp, 1990.

Carman, Taylor. *Heidegger's Analytic: Interpretation, Discourse, and Authenticity in* Being and Time. Cambridge University Press, 2003.

Chomsky, Noam. *Chomsky on Democracy and Education.* Edited by C. P. Otero. New York: RoutledgeFalmer, 2003.

Coltman, Rod. *The Language of Hermeneutics: Gadamer and Heidegger in Dialogue.* New York: State University of New York Press, 1998.

Critchley, Simon, and Reiner Schürmann. *On Heidegger's* Being and Time. Edited by S. Levine. London: Routledge, 2008.

Dahlstrom, O. *Heidegger's Concept of Truth.* Cambridge, Mass: Cambridge University Press, 2001.

Derrida, Jacques. *Aporias.* Translated by Thomas Dutoit. Stanford, Calif.: Stanford University Press, 1993.

———. "Circumfession." In *Jacques Derrida*, by Jacques Derrida and Geoffrey Bennington. Translated by Geoffrey Bennington. Chicago: University of Chicago Press, 1993.

———. *Deconstruction in a Nutshell.* Edited by John D. Caputo. New York: Fordham University Press, 1997.

———. *Dissemination.* Translated by B. Johnson. Chicago: University of Chicago Press, 1981.

———. *The Ear of the Other: Otobiography, Transference, Translation.* Edited by Christie McDonald. Lincoln: University of Nebraska Press, 1985.

———. *Edmund Husserl's Origin of Geometry: An Introduction.* Translated by John P. Leavey Jr. Lincoln: University of Nebraska Press, 1989.

———. "Geschlect II: Heidegger's Hand." In *Deconstruction and Philosophy*, ed.

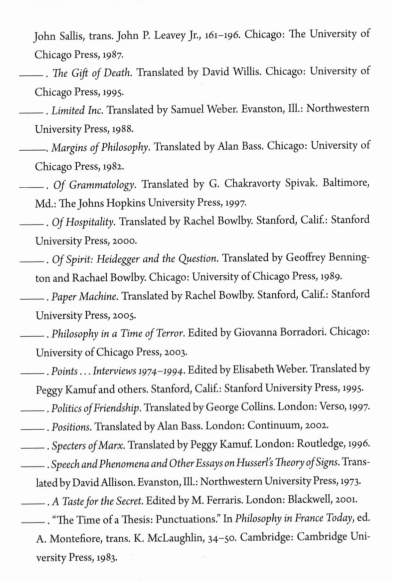

John Sallis, trans. John P. Leavey Jr., 161–196. Chicago: The University of Chicago Press, 1987.

——. *The Gift of Death*. Translated by David Willis. Chicago: University of Chicago Press, 1995.

——. *Limited Inc*. Translated by Samuel Weber. Evanston, Ill.: Northwestern University Press, 1988.

——. *Margins of Philosophy*. Translated by Alan Bass. Chicago: University of Chicago Press, 1982.

——. *Of Grammatology*. Translated by G. Chakravorty Spivak. Baltimore, Md.: The Johns Hopkins University Press, 1997.

——. *Of Hospitality*. Translated by Rachel Bowlby. Stanford, Calif.: Stanford University Press, 2000.

——. *Of Spirit: Heidegger and the Question*. Translated by Geoffrey Bennington and Rachael Bowlby. Chicago: University of Chicago Press, 1989.

——. *Paper Machine*. Translated by Rachel Bowlby. Stanford, Calif.: Stanford University Press, 2005.

——. *Philosophy in a Time of Terror*. Edited by Giovanna Borradori. Chicago: University of Chicago Press, 2003.

——. *Points . . . Interviews 1974–1994*. Edited by Elisabeth Weber. Translated by Peggy Kamuf and others. Stanford, Calif.: Stanford University Press, 1995.

——. *Politics of Friendship*. Translated by George Collins. London: Verso, 1997.

——. *Positions*. Translated by Alan Bass. London: Continuum, 2002.

——. *Specters of Marx*. Translated by Peggy Kamuf. London: Routledge, 1996.

——. *Speech and Phenomena and Other Essays on Husserl's Theory of Signs*. Translated by David Allison. Evanston, Ill.: Northwestern University Press, 1973.

——. *A Taste for the Secret*. Edited by M. Ferraris. London: Blackwell, 2001.

——. "The Time of a Thesis: Punctuations." In *Philosophy in France Today*, ed. A. Montefiore, trans. K. McLaughlin, 34–50. Cambridge: Cambridge University Press, 1983.

———. *The Work of Mourning*. Edited by Pascale-Anne Brault and Michael Nass. Chicago: University of Chicago Press, 2001.

———. *Writing and Difference*. Translated by Alan Bass. Chicago: University of Chicago Press, 1978.

Descombes, Vincent. *The Barometer of Modern Reason: On the Philosophies of Current Events*. Translated by Stephen Adam Schwartz. New York: Oxford University Press, 1993.

Dostal, R. J. *The Cambridge Companion to Gadamer*. Cambridge: Cambridge University Press, 2002.

———, ed. "The Experience of Truth for Gadamer and Heidegger: Taking Time and Sudden Lightning." In *Hermeneutics and Truth*, ed. Brice Wachterhauser, 49–50. Evanston, Ill.: Northwestern University Press, 1994.

Dotolo, C. *La teologia fondamentale davanti alle sfide del 'pensiero deboole di G. Vattimo.'* LAS: Rome 1999.

Dottori, Riccardo. *Die Reflexion des Wirklichen*. Tübingen: Mohr Siebeck, 2006.

Dreyfus, Hubert L. *Being-in-the-World: A Commentary on Heidegger's Being and Time, Division 1*. Cambridge, Mass.: The MIT Press, 1991.

Elliott, Brian. *Phenomenology and Imagination in Husserl and Heidegger*. London: Routledge, 2004.

Esfeld, Michael. "What Heidegger's *Being and Time* Tells Today's Analytic Philosophy." *Philosophical Explorations* 4 (2001): 46–62.

Faulconer, James E., and Mark A. Wrathall, eds. *Appropriating Heidegger*. Cambridge: Cambridge University Press, 2000.

Frascati-Lochhead, Marta. *Kenosis and Feminist Theology: The Challenge of Gianni Vattimo*. New York: State University of New York Press, 1998.

Gadamer, H.-G. *The Beginning of Philosophy*. Translated by Rod Coltman. New York: Continuum, 2001.

———. "Boundaries of Language." In *Language and Linguisticality in Gadamer's*

Hermeneutics, ed. Lawrence K. Schmidt, 9–17. Lanham, Mass.: Lexington Books, 2000.

——— . *A Century of Philosophy: Hans-Georg Gadamer in Conversation with Riccardo Dottori*. Translated by Rod Coltman with Sigrid Koepke. New York: Continuum, 2004.

——— . "Destruktion and Deconstruction," "1. *Letter to Dallmayr*," and "Hermeneutics and Logocentrism," in *Dialogue and Deconstruction: The Gadamer-Derrida Encounter*, ed. D. P. Michelfelder and R. E. Palmer. Albany: State University of New York Press, 1989.

——— . *Das Erbe Europas*. Frankfurt: Suhrkamp, 1989.

——— . "Ethos und Ethik (MacIntyre u. a)." *Philosophische Rundschau* 32 (1985): 1–26.

——— . *Gadamer in Conversation: Reflections and Commentary*. Edited by Richard Palmer. New Haven, Conn.: Yale University Press, 2003.

——— . *The Gadamer Reader: A Bouquet of the Later Writings*. Edited by Jean Grondin. Translated by Richard E. Palmer. Evanston, Ill.: Northwestern University Press, 2007.

——— . *Hans-Georg Gadamer on Education, Poetry, and History: Applied Hermeneutics*. Edited by Dieter Misgeld and Graeme Nicholson. Translated by Lawrence Schmidt and Monica Reuss. Albany: State University of New York Press, 1992.

——— . *Hermeneutics, Religion, and Ethics*. Translated by J. Weinsheimer. New Haven, Conn.: Yale University Press, 1999.

——— . *Philosophical Hermeneutics*. Translated by David E. Linge. Berkeley: University of California Press, 1976.

——— . *The Philosophy of Hans-Georg Gadamer*. Edited by Lewis Edwin Hahn. Library of Living Philosophers 24. Chicago: Open Court Press, 1997.

——— . "Reply to My Critics." In *Hermeneutic Tradition: From Ast to Ricoeur*, ed.

Gayle L. Ormiston and Alan D. Schrift, 273–297. Albany: State University of New York Press, 1990.

———. "Die Stellung der Philosophie in der Gesellschaft." In *Hermeneutik im Rückblick. Gesammelte Werke 10*, 336–372. Tübingen: Mohr Siebeck, 1995.

———. *Truth and Method*. Translated by Joel Weinsheimer and Donald G. Marshall. London: Continuum, 2004.

Gasché, Rodolphe. "Deconstruction and Hermeneutics." In *Deconstructions: A User's Guide*, ed. Nicholas Royle, 137–150. London: Palgrave MacMillan, 2000.

———. *The Tain of the Mirror: Derrida and the Philosophy of Reflection*. Cambridge, Mass.: Harvard University Press, 1986.

———. *Views and Interviews: On 'Deconstruction' in America*. Aurora, Colo.: Davies Group, 2007.

Gilson, Etienne. *Being and Some Philosophers*. Toronto: Pontifical Institute of Mediaeval Studies, 1952.

Giorgio, Giovanni. *Il pensiero di Gianni Vattimo. L'emancipazione dalla metafisica tra dialettica ed ermeneutica*. Milan: Franco Angeli, 2006.

Grondin, Jean. "La contribution silencieuse de Husserl à l'hermeneutique." *Philosophiques* 22 (1993): 383–393.

———. *Hans-Georg Gadamer: A Biography*. Translated by Joel Weinsheimer. New Haven, Conn.: Yale University Press, 2003.

———. "Hermeneutical Truth and Its Historical Presuppositions. A Possible Bridge Between Analysis and Hermeneutics." In *Anti-Foundationalism and Practical Reasoning*, ed. Evan Simpson, 45–58. Edmonton: Academic Printing and Publishing, 1987.

———. *Introduction to Philosophical Hermeneutics*. Translated by Joel Weinsheimer. New Haven, Conn.: Yale University Press, 1994.

———. *The Philosophy of Gadamer*. Montreal: McGill-Queen's University Press, 2003.

———. *Der Sinn der Hermeneutik*. Darmstadt: Wissenschaftliche Buchgesellschaft, 1994.

———. *Sources of Hermeneutics*. Albany: State University of New York Press, 1995.

———. "La thèse de l'herméneutique sur l'être." In *Revue de métaphysique et de morale* 4 (2006): 470–481.

———. *Le tournant dans la pensée de Martin Heidegger*. Paris: Presses Universitaires de France, 1987.

———. "The Tragedies of Understanding in the Analytic and Continental Perspectives." In *Interrogating the Tradition: Hermeneutics and the History of Philosophy*, ed. J. Sallis and J. Scott, 75–83. Albany: State University of New York Press, 2000.

Guignon, Charles. "Being as Appearing: Retrieving the Greek Experience of *Phusis*." In *A Companion to Heidegger's Introduction to Metaphysics*, ed. R. Polt and G. Fried, 34–56. New Haven, Conn.: Yale University Press, 2000.

Habermas, Jürgen. "After Historicism, Is Metaphysics Still Possible?" In *Gadamer's Repercussions: Reconsidering Philosophical Hermeneutics*, ed. Bruce Krajewski, 15–20. Berkeley: University of California Press, 2004.

———. "Hans-Georg Gadamer: Urbanizing the Heideggerian Province." In *Philosophical-Political Profiles*, trans. Frederick Lawrence. Cambridge, Mass.: The MIT Press, 1983.

———. *Postmetaphysical Thinking*. Translated by William M. Hohengarten. Cambridge, Mass.: The MIT Press, 1994.

Harrington, A. *Hermeneutical Dialogue and Social Science: A Critique of Gadamer and Habermas*. London: Routledge, 2001.

Hegel, G. W. F. *Introduction to the Lectures on the History of Philosophy*. Translated by T. M. Knox and A. V. Miller. Oxford: Clarendon Press, 1985.

———. *Science of Logic*. Translated by A. V. Miller. Oxford: Oxford University Press, 1969.

Heidegger, Martin. *Basic Concepts.* Translated by Gary E. Aylesworth. Bloomington: Indiana University Press, 1993.

——. *The Basic Problems of Phenomenology.* Translated by Albert Hofstadter. Bloomington: Indiana University Press, 1982.

——. *Basic Questions of Philosophy: Selected "Problems" of "Logic."* Translated by Richard Rojcewicz and André Schuwer. Bloomington: University of Indiana Press, 1994.

——. *Being and Time.* Translated by Joan Stambaugh. New York: State University of New York Press, 1996.

——. *Contributions to Philosophy (From Enowning).* Translated by Parvis Emad and Kenneth Maly. Bloomington: Indiana University Press, 1999.

——. *Early Greek Thinking.* Translated by D. F. Krell and F. A. Capuzzi. New York: Harper & Row, 1975.

——. *Elucidations of Hölderlin's Poetry.* Translated by Keith Hoeller. New York: Humanity Press, 2000.

——. *The End of Philosophy.* Translated by Joan Stambaugh. New York: Harper & Row, 1973.

——. *The Essence of Human Freedom: An Introduction to Philosophy.* New York: Continuum, 2002.

——. *The Essence of Truth: On Plato's Cave Allegory and Theaetetus.* Translated by Ted Sadler. New York: Continuum, 2001.

——. *Four Seminars: Le Thor 1966, 1968, 1969, Zahringen 1973.* Translated by Andrew Mitchell and Francoise Raffoul. Bloomington: University of Indiana Press, 2003.

——. *Hegel's Phenomenology of Spirit.* Translated by Parvis Emad and Kenneth Maly. Bloomington: University of Indiana Press, 1994.

——. *The Heidegger-Jaspers Correspondence (1920–1963).* Edited by Walter Biemel and Hans Saner. Translated by Gary E. Aylesworth. New York: Humanity Books, 2003.

———. *Introduction to Metaphysics*. Translated by Gregory Fried and Richard Polt. New Haven, Conn.: Yale University Press, 2000.

———. *Identity and Difference*. Translated by Joan Stambaugh. Chicago: University of Chicago Press, 2002.

———. *Kant and the Problem of Metaphysics*. Translated by Richard Raft. Bloomington: University of Indiana Press, 1990.

———. *Logic: The Question of Truth*. Edited by Thomas Sheehan and Corinne Painter. Bloomington: Indiana University Press, forthcoming.

———. *The Metaphysical Foundations of Logic*. Translated by Michael Heim. Bloomington: University of Indiana Press, 1984.

———. *Nietzsche*. Translated by David Farrell Krell. San Francisco: Harper & Row, 1991.

———. *Off the Beaten Track*. Translated by Julian Young and Kenneth Haynes. Cambridge: Cambridge University Press, 2002.

———. *On the Essence of Language: The Metaphysics of Language and the Essencing of the Word; Concerning Herder's Treatise on the Origin of Language*. Translated by Wanda Torres Gregory and Yvonne Unna. New York: State University of New York Press, 2004.

———. *On the Way to Language*. Translated by Peter D. Hertz. New York: Harper & Row, 1982.

———. *On Time and Being*. Translated by B. Johnson. Chicago: University of Chicago Press, 2002.

———. *Ontology: The Hermeneutics of Facticity*. Translated by John van Buren. Bloomington: Indiana University Press, 1999.

———. *Pathmarks*. Edited by William McNeill. Cambridge, Mass.: The MIT Press, 2002.

———. *Phenomenological Interpretations of Aristotle: Initiation Into Phenomenological Research*. Translated by Richard Rojcewicz. Bloomington: University of Indiana Press, 2001.

———. *Philosophical and Political Writings*. Edited by Manfred Stassen. New York: Continuum, 2003.

———. *Poetry, Language, and Thought*. Translated by Albert Hofstadter. New York: Harper & Row, 1971.

———. "Preface." In *Heidegger: Through Phenomenology to Thought*, ed. William Richardson, xiii–xxiii. New York: Fordham University Press, 2003.

———. *The Principle of Reason*. Translated by Reginald Lilly. Bloomington: University of Indiana Press, 1996.

———. *The Question Concerning Technology*. Translated by W. Lovitt. New York: Harper & Row, 1977.

———. *Sojourns: The Journey To Greece*. Translated by John Panteleimon Manoussakis. New York: State University of New York Press, 2005.

———. *What Is Called Thinking?* Translated by J. Glenn Gray. New York: Harper & Row, 1968.

———. *What Is Philosophy?* Translated by Jean T. Wilde and William Kluback. New York: Harper & Row, 2003.

———. *Zollikon Seminars: Protocols—Conversations—Letters*. Edited by Medard Boss. Translated by Franz Mayr and Richard Askay. Evanston, Ill.: Northwestern University Press, 2001.

Heidegger, Martin, and Eugen Fink. *Heraclitus Seminar*. Translated by Charles H. Seibert. Evanston, Ill.: Northwestern University Press, 1993.

Hermann, F. von. *Der Begriff der Phänomenologie in Heidegger und Husserl*. Frankfurt: Vittorio Klostermann Verlag, 1981.

———. "Way and Method: Hermeneutic Phenomenology in Thinking the History of Being." In *Critical Heidegger*, ed. C. Macann, 171–190. London: Routledge, 1996.

Husserl, Edmund. *Ideas Pertaining to a Pure Phenomenology and to a Phenomenological Philosophy: First Book: General Introduction to a Pure Phenomenology*. Translated by F. Kersten. New York: Sprinter, 1983.

——. *Logical Investigations.* Translated by J. N. Findlay. New York: Humanities Press, 1977.

"In Memoriam Reiner Schürmann." *Graduate Faculty Philosophy Journal* 19, no. 2 (1981); 20, no. 1 (1997).

James, Ian. *The Fragmentary Demand: An Introduction to the Philosophy of Jean-Luc Nancy.* Stanford, Calif.: Stanford University Press, 2006.

Keller, Pierre. *Husserl and Heidegger on Human Experience.* Cambridge: Cambridge University Press, 1999.

Kisiel, Theodore. *The Genesis of Heidegger's* Being and Time. Berkeley: University of California Press, 1993.

Krajewski, Bruce, ed. *Gadamer's Repercussions: Reconsidering Philosophical Hermeneutics.* Berkeley: University of California Press, 2004.

Lafont, Cristina. *Heidegger, Language, and World-Disclosure.* Cambridge, Mass.: The MIT Press, 2000.

——. *The Linguistic Turn in Hermeneutic Philosophy.* Cambridge, Mass.: The MIT Press, 1999.

Lawn, C. *Wittgenstein and Gadamer: Towards a Post-Analytic Philosophy of Language.* London: Continuum, 2005.

Lévinas, Emmanuel. *Ethics and Infinity.* Translated by Richard A. Cohen. Pittsburgh, Penn.: Duquesne University Press, 1985.

——. *Existence and Existents.* Translated by Alphonso Lingis. Pittsburgh, Penn.: Duquesne University Press, 2001.

——. "Martin Heidegger and Ontology." *Diacritics* 21, no. 1 (1996): 11–32.

——. *Otherwise Than Being or Beyond Essence.* Translated by Alphonso Lingis. Pittsburgh, Penn.: Duquesne University Press, 2004.

——. *Totality and Infinity: An Essay on Exteriority.* Translated by Alphonso Lingis. Pittsburgh, Penn.: Duquesne University Press, 1969.

Löwith, Karl. *From Hegel to Nietzsche: The Revolution in Nineteenth-Century*

Thought. Translated by David E. Green. New York: Columbia University Press, 1964.

——. *Martin Heidegger and European Nihilism*. Translated by Richard Wolin and Gary Steiner. New York: Columbia University Press, 1998.

——. *Meaning in History: The Theological Implications of the Philosophy of History*. Chicago: University of Chicago Press, 1949.

Lucy, Niall. *A Derrida Dictionary*. Oxford: Blackwell, 2004.

Luther, Martin. *Dr. Martin Luthers Tischreden (1531–46)*. Weimar: Hermann Böhlaus, 1914.

Malpas, J., U. Arnswald, and J. Kertscher, eds. *Gadamer's Century*. Cambridge, Mass.: The MIT Press, 2002.

Marion, Jean-Luc. *Being Given: Toward a Phenomenology of Givenness*. Translated by Jeffrey L. Kosky. Stanford, Calif.: Stanford University Press, 2002.

——. *God Without Being*. Translated by Thomas A. Carlson. Chicago: University of Chicago Press, 1991.

——. *The Idol and Distance*. Translated by Thomas A. Carlson. New York: Fordham University Press, 2001.

——. *In Excess: Studies of Saturated Phenomena*. Translated by Robyn Horner and Vincent Berraud. New York: Fordham University Press, 2002.

——. *Reduction and Givenness: Investigations of Husserl, Heidegger, and Phenomenology*. Translated by T. O. Carlson. Evanston, Ill.: Northwestern University Press, 1998.

Marquet, Jean-Francoise. *Singularité et événement*. Grenoble: Jérome Millon, 1995.

Marrati, P. *Genesis and Trace: Derrida Reading Husserl and Heidegger*. Stanford, Calif.: Stanford University Press, 2005.

Martinengo, Alberto. *Introduzione a Reiner Schürmann*. Rome: Meltemi, 2008.

McNeill, William. *The Glance of the Eye: Heidegger, Aristotle, and the Ends of Theory*. New York: State University of New York Press, 1999.

Nancy, Jean-Luc. *Being Singular Plural*. Translated by Robert D. Richardson. Stanford, Calif.: Stanford University Press, 2000.

——. *The Birth to Presence*. Translated by Brian Holmes and others. Stanford, Calif.: Stanford University Press, 1993.

——. "Ciò che resta di un'arte eterna e fragile." In *Claudio Parmiggiani, Galleria d'Arte Moderna, Bologna. 23 gennaio–30 marzo 2003*, ed. Peter Weiermair, 151–160. Milano: Silvana editoriale.

——. "The Deconstruction of Christianity." In *Religion and Media*, ed. Hent de Vries and Samuel Weber, 112–130. Stanford, Calif.: Stanford University Press, 2001.

——. *The Experience of Freedom*. Translated by Bridget McDonald. Stanford, Calif.: Stanford University Press, 1993.

——. *A Finite Thinking*. Edited by Simon Sparks. Stanford, Calif.: Stanford University Press, 2003.

——. *The Inoperative Community*. Edited by Peter Connor. Minneapolis: University of Minnesota Press, 1991.

——. *The Sense of the World*. Translated by Jeffrey S. Librett. Minneapolis: University of Minnesota Press, 1997.

Newman, Andrew. *The Correspondence Theory of Truth: An Essay on the Metaphysics of Predication*. Cambridge: Cambridge University Press, 2002.

Nietzsche, Friedrich. *On the Genealogy of Morals*. Dover: Dover Publications: 2003.

Ormiston, Gayle L., and Alan D. Schrift, eds. *The Hermeneutic Tradition: From Ast to Ricoeur*. New York: State University of New York Press, 1990.

——, eds. *Transforming the Hermeneutic Context: From Nietzsche to Nancy*. New York: State University of New York Press, 1990.

Palmer, Richard. *Hermeneutics: Interpretation Theory in Schleiermacher, Dilthey, Heidegger, and Gadamer.* Evanston, Ill.: Northwestern University Press, 1969.

Pareyson, Luigi. *Essere, Libertà, Ambiguità.* Edited by F. Tomatis. Milan: Mursia, 1998.

——. *Ontologia della libertà. Il male e la sofferenza.* Turin: Einaudi, 1995.

Pippin, R. P. *Modernism as a Philosophical Problem: On the Dissatisfactions of European High Culture.* Cambridge, Mass.: Blackwell, 1991.

Pöggeler, Otto. *Heidegger und die Hermeneutische Philosophie.* Freiburg: Alber, 1983.

Rapaport, Herman, *Heidegger and Derrida: Reflections on Time and Language.* Lincoln: University of Nebraska Press, 1991.

Richardson, William. *Heidegger: Through Phenomenology to Thought.* New York: Fordham University Press, 2003.

Ricoeur, Paul. *The Conflict of Interpretations.* Edited by Don Ihde. London: Continuum, 1974.

——. *From Text to Action: Essays in Hermeneutics II.* Translated by Kathleen Blamey and John B. Thompson. Evanston, Ill.: Northwestern University Press, 1991.

——. *Hermeneutics and the Human Sciences: Essays on Language, Action, and Interpretation.* Edited by John B. Thompson. Cambridge: Cambridge University Press, 1981.

——. *Interpretation Theory: Discourse and the Surplus of Meaning.* Texas: Christian University Press, 1976.

——. *Memory, History, Forgetting.* Translated by K. Blamey and D. Pellauer. Chicago: University of Chicago Press, 2004.

——. *Oneself as Another.* Translated by Kathleen Blamey. Chicago: University of Chicago Press, 1992.

Ricoeur, Paul, and Hans-Georg Gadamer. "The Conflict of Interpretation." In

Phenomenology: Dialogue and Bridges, ed. R. Bruzina and B. Wilshire, 299–320. Albany: State University of New York Press, 1982.

Riera, Gabriel, ed. *Alain Badiou: Philosophy and Its Conditions.* Albany: State University of New York Press, 2005.

Risser, James. *Hermeneutics and the Voice of the Other: Re-reading Gadamer's Philosophical Hermeneutics.* Albany: State University of New York Press, 1997.

Rorty, Richard, and Gianni Vattimo. *The Future of Religion.* Edited by Santiago Zabala. New York: Columbia University Press, 2005.

Sallis, John. *Delimitations: Phenomenology and the End of Metaphysics.* Bloomington: Indiana University Press, 1986, 1995.

Schürmann, Reiner. *Broken Hegemonies.* Translated by R. Lilly. Bloomington: University of Indiana Press, 2003.

——— . "Deconstruction Is Not Enough. On Gianni Vattimo's Call for Weak Thinking." *Graduate Faculty Philosophy Journal* 10 (1984): 165–177.

——— . *On Being and Acting: From Principles to Anarchy.* Translated by C.-M. Gros. Bloomington: University of Indiana Press, 1990.

——— . "Questioning the Foundations of Practical Philosophy." In *Phenomenology: Dialogues and Bridges,* ed. R. Bruzina, and B. Wilshire, 11–21. Albany: State University of New York Press, 1982.

——— . "Symbolic Difference." *Graduate Faculty Philosophy Journal* 19 (1997): 9–38.

Sheehan, Thomas. "Heidegger." In *The Shorter Routledge Encyclopedia of Philosophy,* ed. Edward Craig, 359. London: Routledge, 2005.

——— . "Husserl and Heidegger: The Making and Unmaking of a Relationship." In *Psychological and Transcendental Phenomenology and the Confrontation with Heidegger, 1927–1931,* by E. Husserl, trans. T. Sheehan and R. Palmer, 1–32. Dordrecht: Kluwer Academic Publishers, 1997.

Steiner, George. *Lessons of the Masters.* Cambridge, Mass.: Harvard University Press, 2005.

——. *Martin Heidegger*. Chicago: University of Chicago Press, 1991.

Stellardi, Giuseppe. *Heidegger and Derrida on Philosophy and Metaphor: Imperfect Thought*. London: Prometheus, 2000.

Stenstad, Gail. *Transformations: Thinking After Heidegger*. Madison: University of Wisconsin Press, 2005.

Stocker, Barry, *Routledge Philosophy Guidebook to Derrida on Deconstruction*. London: Routledge, 2006.

Theunissen, Michael. *The Other: Studies in the Social Ontology of Husserl, Heidegger, Sartre, and Bubner*. Cambridge, Mass.: The MIT Press, 1986.

——. "Philosophische Hermeneutik als Phänomenologie der Traditionsaneignung." In *Sein, das verstanden Werden kann, ist Sprache*, 61–88. Frankfurt: Suhrkamp, 2001.

——. *Sein und Schein. Die kritische Funktion der Hegelschen Logik*. Frankfurt: M. Suhrkamp, 1978.

Tugendhat, Ernst. "The Dissolution of Ontology Into Formal Semantics." In *The Hermeneutic Nature of Analytic Philosophy: A Study of Ernst Tugendhat*, by S. Zabala, 98–106. New York: Columbia University Press, 2008.

——. "Existence in Space and Time." In *Philosophische Aufsätze*, 67–89. Frankfurt: Suhrkamp, 1992.

——. "The Fusion of Horizons. A Review of Hans-Georg Gadamer, *Truth and Method* and *Philosophical Hermeneutics*." *Times Literary Supplement* (May 19, 1978). Also in E. Tugendhat, *Philosophische Aufsätze*, 426–432. Frankfurt: Suhrkamp, 1992.

——. "Language Analysis and the Critique of Ontology." In *Contemporary German Philosophy*, ed. Darrel E. Christensen, 2:100–111. State College: Penn State University Press, 1983.

——. "Heidegger's Idea of Truth." In *Hermeneutics and Truth*, ed. Brice Wachterhauser, 83–97. Northwestern University Press, 1994.

——. "Phenomenology and Linguistic Analysis." In *Husserl: Expositions and*

Appraisals, ed. F. Elliston and P. McCormick. Notre Dame, Ind.: University of Notre Dame Press, 1977.

——. "The Question About Being and Its Foundation in Language (on Charles H. Kahn, 'The Verb 'Be' In Ancient Greek')." In *Contemporary German Philosophy,* ed. Darrel E. Christensen, 3:259–270. State College: Penn State University Press, 1983.

——. *Self-Consciousness and Self-Determination.* Translated by Paul Stern. Cambridge, Mass.: The MIT Press, 1986.

——. *Traditional and Analytical Philosophy: Lectures on the Philosophy of Language.* Cambridge: Cambridge University Press, 1982.

Vattimo, Gianni. *The Adventure of Difference: Philosophy After Nietzsche and Heidegger.* Translated by C. P. Blamires and T. Harrison. Cambridge: Polity Press, 1993.

——. *After Christianity.* Translated by L. D'Isanto. New York: Columbia University Press, 2002.

——. *Beyond Interpretation: The Meaning of Hermeneutics for Philosophy.* Translated by D. Webb. Cambridge: Polity Press, 1997.

——. "Bottle, Net, Truth, Revolution, Terrorism, Philosophy." *Denver Quarterly* 16 (1982): 24–34.

——. "Dialectics, Difference, and Weak Thought." *Graduate Faculty Philosophy Journal* 10 (1984): 151–163.

——. "Diritto all'argomentazione." In *Filosofia '92,* ed. G. Vattimo, 59–70. Rome-Bari: Laterza, 1993.

——. *The End of Modernity: Nihilism and Hermeneutics in Postmodern Culture.* Translated by J. R. Snyder. Baltimore, Md.: The John Hopkins University Press, 1988.

——. *Essere, storia e linguaggio in Heidegger.* Genoa: Marietti: 1989.

——. "Foreword." In *The Hermeneutic Nature of Analytic Philosophy: A Study of Ernst Tugendhat,* by S. Zabala, xi–xvii. New York: Columbia University Press, 2007.

———. "Gadamer and the Problem of Ontology." In *Gadamer's Century,* ed. J. Malpas, U. Arnswald, and J. Kertscher, 299–306. Cambridge, Mass.: The MIT Press, 2002.

———. "Nietzsche and Heidegger." In *Stanford Italian Review* 6 (1986): 19–29.

———. *Nihilism and Emancipation: Ethics, Politics, and Law.* Edited by Santiago Zabala. Translated by William McCuaig. New York: Columbia University Press, 2004.

———. "Ontology of Actuality." In *Contemporary Italian Philosophy,* ed. S. Benso and B. Schroeder, 87–107. New York: State University of New York Press, 2007.

———. "Pensiamo in compagnia." *L'espresso* 45 (November 8, 2001): 193.

———. "Toward an Ontology of Decline." In *Recoding Metaphysics: The New Italian Philosophy,* ed. G. Borradori. Evanston, Ill.: Northwestern University Press, 1988.

———. " 'Weak Thought' and the Reduction of Violence. A Dialogue with Gianni Vattimo by Santiago Zabala." *Common Knowledge* 3 (2002): 452–463.

Vattimo, Gianni, and Pier Aldo Rovatti, eds. *Il pensiero debole.* Milan: Feltrinelli, 1983.

Wachterhauser, Brice R., ed. *Hermeneutics and Truth.* Evanston, Ill.: Northwestern University Press, 1994.

Wheeler, Samuel C. *Deconstruction as Analytic Philosophy.* Stanford, Calif.: Stanford University Press, 2000.

Wittgenstein L., *Philosophical Investigations.* Translated by G. E. M. Ascombe. Oxford: Basil Blackwell, 1953.

———. *Tractatus Logico-Philosophicus.* Translated by D. F. Pears and B. F. McGuinness. London: Routledge, 2001.

Wolin, Richard. *Heidegger's Children: Hannah Arendt, Karl Löwith, Hans Jonas, and Herbert Marcuse*. Princeton, N.J.: Princeton University Press, 2001.

——. *The Heidegger Controversy: A Critical Reader*. New York: Columbia University Press, 1991. 2nd ed., Cambridge, Mass.: The MIT Press, 1993.

——. *The Politics of Being*. New York: Columbia University Press, 1992.

Wrathall, M. "Heidegger and Truth as Correspondence." *International Journal of Philosophical Studies* 7 (1999): 79–88.

Wright, Kathleen, ed. *Festivals of Interpretation: Essays on Hans-Georg Gadamer's Work*. New York: State University of New York Press, 1990.

Zabala, Santiago. "Ending the Rationality of Faith Through Interpretation." *Sensus Communis* 5, no. 4, issue 14 (September–December 2004): 422–439.

——. *The Hermeneutic Nature of Analytic Philosophy: A Study of Ernst Tugendhat*. Translated by Michael Haskell and Santiago Zabala. New York: Columbia University Press, 2008.

——. "Pharmakons of Onto-theology." In *Weakening Philosophy: Essays in Honour of Gianni Vattimo*, ed. S. Zabala. Montreal: McGill-Queen's University Press, 2007.

INDEX

Abbau, 28

abyss, 59

actuality, ontology of, 92–93, 124n. 22

aletheiological constellations, 61, 63, 73

anarchies, economical, 58–66

an-archism, 104, 106–8, 118

Andenken, 97

Anwesenheit, 30, 59, 61, 68–69. *See also* presence

appropriation, 45–49, 55, 62, 64–65, 102

Aquinas, Thomas, xiii

Aristotle, xiii, 30, 59, 92, 106

Aufhebung (elevation), 46–47, 117

authority, 33, 68

becoming, 54, 65, 95–96, 102–3

Being: concealments of, 39–40, 42, 61, 63; Dasein as relation to, 32–35, 38, 40, 100; destiny of, 55, 67, 69–70, 94, 135n. 55; determined by time as presence, 26, 30–31, 38, 42, 46, 53; disclosure of, 95; dissolution of, 96–97; as event, xi, 52, 59, 65–66, 93–95, 104, 109; finitude of, 73–74; genitive of, 26, 43–44, 51;

Being (*continued*):

grammatical categories of, 26–27; guardianship of, 41, 44, 51, 67; human beings as sayers, 30, 35; intrinsic understanding of, 35–36; originary, 51, 53–55, 64–65, 72; reason and, 54, 56, 93, 95–96; thought of, 54–55, 100; tidings of, 32–33, 51, 103, 118; understanding and, 85–87; working out of, 27, 36, 39, 52, 54, 56–57, 78, 92, 101, 116. *See also* destruction of Being; generation of Being; meaning of Being; oblivion of Being; ontological difference; question of Being; thinking of Being; understanding of Being; weak Being; worn-out Being

Being and Time (Heidegger), 25, 26, 54, 85, 100; destructuring of history of ontology, 29–30, 40; hermeneutical relation in, 32–33, 40; plan of, 45; on presence and time, 30–31. *See also* Heidegger, Martin

being-in-the-world, 37, 82, 96

Being-relationship, 38

being (*seiend*), 36

being-singular-plural, 76

Being Singular Plural (Nancy), 75–78

being-with, 76–77

being-with-one-another-in-the-world, 77

belonging, 115

Bersgon, Henri, xiii

Beyond Interpretation (Vattimo), 98

biblical texts, 113–14

birth, 74

Bruns, Gerald L., 102–3, 125n. 28

canons, 60

cause, 31

certainty, search for, 31–32, 46–47

classical, the, 113–14

coessence, 75–76

cogito, 44

community, 78–79

constellation of events, 59–66, 73

constellations, aletheiological, 61, 63, 73

conversation, 26, 80–82, 116

conversations of language, 78–86, 109

copresences of singular plurals, 72–78, 109

copula, 91–92

correspondence theory of truth, 54

Dasein, 135n. 53, 137n. 98, 138n. 5; as being-in-the-world, 37; as Being of human being, 30; as guardianship of Being, 51; as hermeneutical relation, 32–35, 38, 40, 100; as historical, 38–39, 107; as

in-between, 117–18; ontological difference and, 36–38; self-understanding,
85; singular-plural and, 77–78; task of
to work out Being, 52; as term, 133n.
35; as thrown project, 110–11. *See also*
existence

decline, philosophy of, 93

deconstruction, 28, 58–59, 64, 73–74;
end of, 94; as thinking of Being,
67–68

Derrida, Jacques, xiii, 28, 57, 109, 131n.
20; *différance*, 70–72, 74, 84, 104. *See
also* trace

Descartes, René, xiii, 31–32, 33, 44

Descombes, Vincent, 123–24n. 22, 124n.
22, 125n. 28

destiny of Being, 55, 67, 69–70, 94–95,
135n. 55

destruction of Being, xiii; *Destruktion*, as
term, 26–28, 40, 131–32n. 20; discussion as, 39–40; goal of, 27–28; Schürmann's view, 58–59; tradition and,
40–41

dialogue, 26, 39–40, 80–81

dichotomies, xiv, 28–29, 31, 36

différance, 70–72, 74, 84, 104

difference between Being and beings. *See*
ontological difference

discursive continuities, logics of, 104–11,
112, 115

dissolution of Being, 96–97, 105

economical anarchies, traits of, 58–66,
108–9

effect (*Erwirkung*), 37

ego, 31–33

emergence, synchronic, 62

epochs in history of philosophy, xii–xiii,
59, 62, 108–9, 140n. 21; postmetaphysical, xiv, 58, 61, 63, 93; representations of
Being and, 60; self-regulation, 65–66.
See also presencing; time

essence, 31, 36, 42, 47

ethics, 129n. 3

event, Being as, xi, 52, 59, 65–66, 93–95,
104, 109

events: constellation of, 59–60; of weakness, 92–98

existence, xi–xii, 31, 36, 38, 41, 74–75, 100,
133n. 35; folding of, 71, 73, 75. *See also*
Dasein

existent, 91

experience, 114–15

fallenness, 34, 80, 133n. 35, 36

family resemblance, 111

105; as interpretation from within, 97–98, 107, 111–12; as philosophy of generation, 99, 111–12, 115–16

history of Being, 27–28, 32, 38–39, 46, 52, 70, 94; generation of Being and, 104, 106–8, 118

Hölderlin, Friedrich, 119

Husserl, Edmund, 44

incorporation, 57, 67–68, 101–2

interpretation, 56, 58, 83–84; from within, 97–98, 107, 111–12; generation of Being and, 100, 101, 104–5, 115–16; ground of, 116–17; knowledge as, 96; productive, 104–5

Kant, Immanuel, xiii

Kierkegaard, Søren, 129n. 3

kinesis, 106–8, 115

language, 45, 51, 66–67, 129n. 3; conversations of, 78–86, 109; factualness, 81–82; human beings as sayers, 30, 35; inseparable from thinking, 82–83; meanings of sentences, 86–92; objects and, 86–88; remains of Being preserved in, 55–56; thinking with, 84; unthought, 53

"Language Analysis and the Critique of Ontology" (Tugendhat), 86

language-analytical reflection, 88–89

Lévinas, Emmanuel, xi

linguistic signs, 88

logics of discursive continuities, 104–11, 112, 115

logos, 30, 82, 106, 107, 118

Luther, Martin, 26, 113–14

meaning of Being, 53–54; as historical inquiry, 38–39; retrieving, 29–41

meanings of sentences, 86–92

metaphysics, xii; as history of oblivion of Being, 31–32, 69–70; intrinsic nature of, 29–30; language of, 45; neglect of language-analytical reflection, 88–89. *See also* overcoming of metaphysics

Mitsein, 77–78

Nancy, Jean-Luc, xiv–xv, 57, 72–78, 109, 131–32n. 20

Nietzsche, Friedrich, xiii, xiv, 47, 49, 97

nihilism, 97

Nihilism and Emancipation (Vattimo), 92–93, 125n. 28

noein, 30, 90

nominalization, 31, 89, 91

nothingness of Being, xiv, 29, 48, 97. *See also* oblivion of Being

nous, 106, 107

objectiveness, 26, 30, 40–41; science/technology and, 33–34, 44–45

objects: language and, 86–88; subjective command over, 62–63

oblivion of Being, xi, 26, 39, 69, 132–33n. 33; metaphysics as history of, 31–32, 69–70; originary Being and, 53–55

Of Grammatology (Derrida), 66

ontological difference, 25, 31, 36–39, 42–43, 68–73, 79, 100, 134n. 42; appropriation of, 45–49; becoming and, 95–96; originary Being and, 54–55, 72; securing foundations, 59–60; trace and, 68–69

ontology: of actuality, 92–93, 124n. 22; traditional, 40–41, 59, 68–69, 72–73, 85–89, 106–7, 114–16

ontology of remnants, 58, 92–93, 99, 103–5, 112–13, 118–19. *See also* remains of Being

overcoming of metaphysics, xiii–xiv, 31, 42, 45–46, 55; coming to terms with metaphysics, 79–80; consequences of, 58; generation of Being and, 101–2

Parmenides, xi, 30

Pippin, Robert B., 54

Plato, xiii, 47, 81–82; beginning of metaphysics in, 31, 123n. 10; *Sophist*, 36; *Symposium*, 102–3

Pöggeler, Otto, 54

possible/possibility, 38, 71–73

postmetaphysical epoch, xiv, 58, 61, 63, 93

predicate, 90–92

presence: actuality, ontology of, 92–93, 124n. 22; as anarchic economy, 62; as *Anwesenheit*, 30, 59, 61, 68–69; Being determined as time by, 26, 30–31, 38, 42, 46, 53; constellation of events, 59–66, 73; copresences of singular plurals, 72–78; destruction of Being as, xiii; objective, 30; objective (*Vorhandenheit*), 30, 40–41, 89; time and, 30–31; trace and, 68–70

presencing, 31, 59; absencing and, 62–63, 66. *See also* epochs in history of philosophy

projects, 96, 110–11

"Question About Being and Its Foundation in Language, The" (Tugendhat), 86–92

question of Being, xii, 35; Dasein and, 34,

38–40; "how is it going with Being?" 49–50, 57–58, 72, 86, 93, 105–6, 122n. 8

rationality, 33–34

reason, 34, 54, 56, 93, 95–96

reflexion, 44

remain, as term, 105

remains of Being, xi, xiii–xiv; effects as, 113–14; encounter with, 114–15; existence and, 74–75; generation and, 58, 102–3; preserved in language, 55–56, 78–86; six varieties of, 56–57; trace, 55–56. *See also* ontology of remnants

repetition, 26, 39, 49–50

representation, 33, 60, 90

result/present residue, 56

Rorty, Richard, 114

Sachverhalte (matters of fact), 81–82

Schürmann, Reiner, xiv, 57, 93, 104, 107–9, 118; traits of economical anarchies, 58–66, 140n. 21

science and technology, 35; objectivistic nature, 33–34, 44–45; ontological difference and, 36–37

seeing, metaphor of, 87

self-regulation, epochal, 65–66

self-relationship, 38

self-understanding, 40–41, 42–43

semantics, formal, 87–88

sentences: affirmation and negation, 89–90; copula, 91–92; meanings of, 86–92, 110; predicate, 90–92

singular plurals, copresences of, 72–78, 109

social divisions, 34

speech (*rede*), 106–7

Stambaugh, Joan, 46

status, 109

statutus, 109

subject, 26, 31–33, 133n. 35

subjectum, 31

substantives, 89

Symposium (Plato), 102–3

thinking: *Andenken*, 97; difficulty of, 100–101; economic, 140n. 21; with language, 84; language inseparable from, 82–83; weak thought, 93

thinking of Being, 44–47, 65–66, 73–74; deconstruction as, 67–68

third-person-singular, 27, 33, 122n. 7

thrownness, 34, 54, 96, 110–11, 133n. 35, 36

time: Being determined as presence by, 26, 30–31, 38, 42, 46, 53; being-in-the-time (*continued*):

world, 37; presence and, 30–31. *See also* epochs in history of philosophy

trace, xiii, 55–56, 64, 66–72, 109, 142n. 63; *différance*, 70–72, 74, 84, 104; ontological difference and, 68–69

traditional ontology, 40–41, 59, 68–69, 72–73, 85–89, 106–7, 114–16

traits of economical anarchies, 58–66, 140n. 21

trans-mission, 94–95

truth, 54, 102, 138n. 2; aletheiological constellations, 61, 63, 73; conversation and, 84

Truth and Method (Gadamer), 81–82

Tugendhat, Ernst, xv, 57, 94, 146n. 141; meanings of sentences, 86–92, 110

understanding of Being, 73, 79–80, 85–87; interpretation and, 83–84, 112; meanings of sentences and, 86–87

Vattimo, Gianni, xv, 54, 103–4, 108, 112, 118, 146–47n. 144; *Beyond Interpreta-* *tion*, 98; *Nihilism and Emancipation*, 92–93; productive interpretation, 104–5

Verwindung, 45, 79–80, 93

Vorhandenheit (objective presence), 30, 40–41, 89

Vorliegende, 31–32

war, 132–33n. 33

weak Being, xiii–xiv, 92–98, 103–4, 118–19. *See also* worn-out Being

weakness, events of, 92–98

Wiederholung (repetition, retrieval), 39

will to power, 97

Wittgenstein, Ludwig, 25, 100, 111, 129n. 3

Wolf, Christian, xii

worn-out Being, xiii, 41–52, 55–57, 56, 108. *See also* conversations of language; copresences of singular plurals; events, of weakness; meanings of sentences; trace; traits of economical anarchies; weak Being